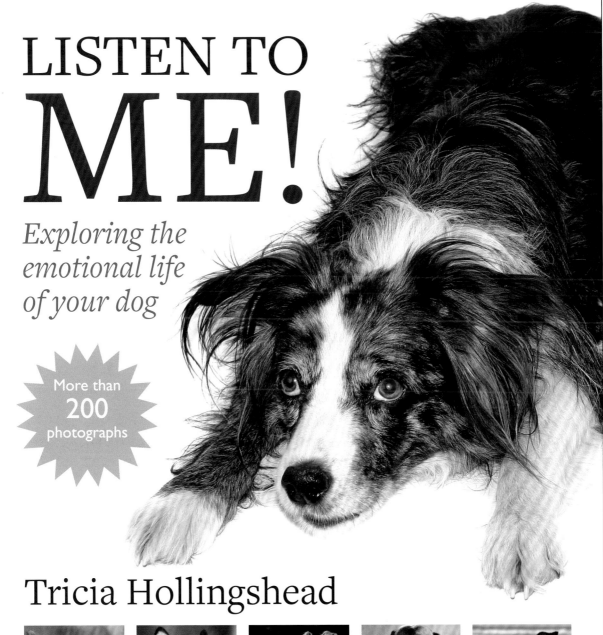

LISTEN TO ME!

Exploring the emotional life of your dog

More than **200** photographs

Tricia Hollingshead

'A wonderful book'
SARAH FISHER

'Really amazing'
TURID RUGAAS

This book is dedicated to:
The owner of every dog I have ever had contact with....

ACKNOWLEDGEMENTS

Theresa Toomey and Ali Scott – to have best friends who are also colleagues is a huge pleasure; to have the best colleagues out there be my best friends is an honour. Your belief that I had something special to say was inspiring.

Marcus, Theresa, Penny, Dolores, Paula, Sharon, Georgina and my Mum: Many thanks for your feedback and support. And to Claire for her typing skills.

To Julia, editor extraordinaire – thank you.

The owners who let us photograph the sometimes not so pretty aspects of their relationships with their dogs. Very few people are that generous – thank you so much.

All my stooges, especially: Alison, Oli, Jenny, Peter, Maxine, Carol, Jayne and Kate who helped out on photo shoot days. I am also hugely indebted to all the stooges and their dogs who have worked with me, over the years, to build up the confidence of so many dogs. Particularly Jayne, Ali and Abby and also optimistic-to-the-end Barbara and cake-making Penny, sadly both now deceased, but certainly not forgotten.

To Justin and Maeve, now young adults with a beautiful sensitivity to dogs, and to my Dad, now deceased, who took quite a few of the photographs.

To my husband, Marcus, my photo librarian and retriever of all thing lost on the laptop. My provider of food for body and soul. More than anything I appreciate your consistent gentleness with every dog that shares our home.

To Sarah Heath and Turid Rugaas who gave me the opportunity to work with them and learn from them.

I am the luckiest dog lover in the world – people let me look after and help train their precious dogs. To all these people, it is your dogs that have inspired, nurtured and challenged my understanding of the best being in the world – a dog. A multi million thanks!

First published in 2020 by First Stone Publishing, an imprint of Westline Publishing Limited, The Old Hen House, St Martin's Farm, Zeals, Warminster BA12 6NZ United Kingdom.

ISBN 978 1 910488 55 3

Cover and interior design: Alan Cooper

Printed through Printworks Global Ltd

1 2 3 4 5 6 7 8 9 0

FOREWORD
Turid Rugaas

Congratulations Tricia! Your book, so long thought about, and planned in such detail, is now here...

When I read the manuscript, it took me back to the many hours we spent walking in the forests around my farm, accompanied by my dog, discussing and talking about dogs – what else?

As we talked, I became increasingly impressed by your views on dog behaviour, which combine an eye for detail, an in-depth knowledge of the subject, and a very practical approach to solving problems. It is such a pleasure to read your book and to discover that my impressions from that time in Norway were right. You have a gift for observing behaviour which gives us an insight into the emotional life of dogs.

Dogs have such have a varied and detailed communication system, but problems are quick to arise when we fail to understand what they are communicating. This book will be a great help in learning how to see our dogs, and understand what they are telling us.

It is a whole adventure seeing such descriptive photos following the relevant text, which also makes it such a pleasure to read. The result is really amazing. I hope many dog owners will read and enjoy it as much as I did.

Turid Rugaas is an internationally-renowned trainer, who has revealed the secrets of canine communication to the dog world. In her best-selling book, On Talking Terms With Dogs, she has identified social skills, known as 'calming signals' that have revolutionised our understanding of dog behaviour. Turid, who lives in Norway, is a highly sought after speaker and has conducted seminars and workshops and lectures in 34 different countries, and counting...

EVERY PICTURE TELLS A STORY
A simple head turn communicates a wealth of different feelings.

1. These two dogs are having a casual conversation that involves a subtle head turn.
2. The Shar-Pei (right) uses a head turn as part of a non-threatening negotiation.
3. The Beagle uses a head turn to peacefully avoid the puppy's pestering.
4. Perhaps the basis of the head turn behaviour, used here, is to avoid being bitten.
5. To avoid provoking the Tibetan Terrier (front), the Leonberger turns his head while also taking a curved path.

Our dogs have never had it so good. In today's world food and shelter are provided, there are no threats from predators, and there is not even the need to make decisions. The domesticated dog has found a place as a much-loved and cared for member of the family circle. So why are so many dogs suffering from stress and anxiety?

Formerly, behaviourists were called in to tackle problems resulting from poor breeding, neglect, or lack of socialisation and training. But increasingly it is the pet dog, supposedly living without a care in the world, that is in trouble. There are dogs who have a phobia about being left on their own; those who cannot tolerate being groomed or going to the vet. There are dogs who are swamped by the well-meaning attentions of their family, terrified of the family cat, or bullied by another dog in the same household.

The everyday routines that we create in order to instill a sense of security can, instead, be a nightmare for the misunderstood dog. Where are we going wrong? Our pet dogs do astonishingly well at accommodating us; the older they get the more they seem to fit snugly into our lives. We take this for granted, making demands which may seem very unnatural and sometimes stressful to a dog. But what effort do we make to understand a dog's emotional state? We have the benefit of our superior knowledge and intelligence, which we can enhance by reading, talking, internet research, watching dvds and attending seminars.

A dog has no such support. His perception of situations, and his reactions are rooted in his genetic make up and his emotional outlook. He is constantly sending out signals that let us know how he is feeling, but are we picking them up?

Of course you will never know exactly what your dog is feeling, any more than you know exactly what your friend or partner is thinking at any particular time. However, you read facial expressions and take account of the context, which will enable you to make a very good guess. With your dog the chance of working out what is going on is even greater because

Perceiving his playmate's change of mood, this dog settles nearby and, tentatively, makes nose and paw contact. This awareness of human emotions is most endearing.

he rarely bluffs and doesn't lie; his mental processes are not as complicated as the human psyche. With increasing experience, your awareness will improve as you learn what is 'normal' behaviour for your dog, what excites or worries him, and how he has been affected by previous experiences. This will make a massive difference to your dog; you will be able to avoid situations he finds difficult or moderate your behaviour so that he doesn't have to become stressed.

Living with a dog is a two-way street and as you try to work out how your dog is feeling, he is also trying to pick up on your emotions. Because we value our dogs so highly, we are prone to over-estimate their aptitude for seeing life as we do. In reality, a dog has only the minutest ability to view the world from a human perspective. He has no idea of who we are or what we do beyond his direct experience of us. If this experience is inconsistent, unpredictable and, at times, unfathomable, how can a dog ever learn to relax?

A dog is on red alert, watching his people and mirroring their moods. He is not empathetic in the sense that he understands what his people are thinking or feeling, but he will reflect their behaviour. For example, if you are quiet and subdued, he will tone down his behaviour; if you are hyped up and excited, he will rush around the house barking and wagging his tail. He is not sad or excited for the same reasons as you are, but he appears to share your emotion as he reacts to the changes he has observed. Even if you think you are masking your emotions, your dog will sense the subtlest of changes in body language.

Unlike humans, dogs rely very much more on the here and now. A dog is quick to forgive and forget and does not carry the emotional baggage of regret and guilt that we lug around. His commitment to living in the present is endearing, but there is a price to pay. Inevitably, he is swept along with the emotional framework that we provide. He has to deal with arousal/boredom, contentment/anxiety, consistency/inconsistency, security/insecurity – no wonder he sometimes finds that life is a confusing business.

WHAT CAN YOU DO?

First of all, we need to understand what we humans have done in creating the domesticated dog. All the hundreds of dog breeds we recognise today are descended from wolves, but there is a vast difference between the wild wolf who lives in a pack and hunts for food, and the domesticated dog curled up at your feet. For the most part, your dog has lost the ability – and more importantly, the opportunity – to hunt for his food.

He needs a human to prepare his food, to fill his water bowl and to let him in and out to toilet. In all practical matters, we have made him dependent on us and although he plays an active part in the relationship, providing love and companionship, the balance of control in this partnership is clearly tipped in our direction.

The degree to which your dog is dependent on you is easy to overlook and, unlike children, this does not decrease with the passage of time. Even when your dog is fully mature, he is unable to wash his bedding or make his own supper. He won't ever get a job and leave home. For the whole of his life he needs you to care for him, to provide pleasure and entertainment, to protect him from danger, and to be his voice, translating for him when he is in pain or discomfort and needs help from a professional. The benefits for a dog are tangible, but is such dependency always in his interests?

A dog cannot change his situation and so what is happening within the family circle is of paramount importance. It affects his everyday existence – whether he is going for a walk or when he is going to be fed – but, more importantly, it affects his mental wellbeing.

Domestication has changed his outlook, and although he enjoys canine company, it is the people in his life that have the greater significance. A dog has nothing else to do but to follow your every movement. Day in, day out, you have a hundred different things to do and think about, but a dog's overriding preoccupation is trying to work out what you are going to do next. If you go near to where a lead is kept, does that signal a walk is in the offing? If you go to a cupboard, does that mean food could be on its way? Or does a change in your tone of voice mean you are ready for a game? Your dog has the time to observe everything you do, and he becomes expert at interpreting the slightest change in your body language and the differences in sequences and patterns of your routines. This happens to the extent that you feel as though he knows what you are thinking.

The focus of a dog's daily life is where his people are and, given free range of the house, he will nearly always choose to be with his family. In the evenings, when everyone sits down to watch television, that is where the dog will be and, at night, when everyone goes to bed, most dogs would rather be allowed upstairs with you. The contented dog falls into the rhythm of our lives, picking up the clues which will tell him what is going to happen next, and what he should be doing to fit in.

The flip side of this dependent existence is when there is a breakdown in order or structure. His people appear to behave unpredictably and when they interact with him, he does not feel comfortable. He adopts a coping strategy such as responding to rough play or giving an over-the-top greeting after hours of separation. But what is he feeling? Does he feel comfortable playing rough-house with you? Is he really excited to see you when you return home? Or could it be that he is offering behaviours that get him out of jail? Is he responding in a confident, relaxed manner or is his behaviour affected by a high degree of stress?

What is this puppy communicating?

Although this puppy is jumping up, she is not trying to say "hello". Her head and ears are held back, her mouth is tense, and she is looking away into space, wanting to avoid the present situation.

When she finds no relief, the dropped tail, hunched back, head pulled back, wide eyes and tight lips make her plight more obvious.

IMPROVING YOUR UNDERSTANDING

A dog will do everything in his power to fit in with your lifestyle, sharing activities conforming to your rules, and sharing your emotions. So what can you do to make his life easier?

The most effective way of opening up communication is to monitor a dog's facial expressions and body language. It is the dogs with the more severe behavioural problems that send out the clearest, most blatant signals. If you witness the body language that a troubled dog uses in an extreme situation, it is very obvious which emotions are involved. During the process of rehabilitation, both the emotion and the body language become less extreme and may even reach a level of subtlety.

For the behaviourist, this is something to be celebrated and useful information is gained about the lowering of emotional arousal by watching the gradual dilution of signaling and communication. But for the pet owner with a less extreme or more normal dog, it can be difficult to read the subtler signs which tell you how your dog is feeling. In reality, you may be doing better than you think. When you observe your dog, you will be deducing how he is feeling – even if you are doing it sub-consciously.

Do you know your dog's favourite person/walk/ game? Do you know where he likes to be rubbed or stroked when you are petting him? If so, you have come to those conclusions because of the differences in his body language. You may not have consciously identified the clues he is giving you, but you are already practised in quantifying his emotional investment.

Do you find yourself explaining his behaviour in terms of dilemmas?

"He's very good and puts up with it, but he doesn't really like it..."

"He does it, but it's as if he doesn't really want to..."

"He acts all confident, but really he's scared..."

You can see the emotional conflict and the resulting stress he experiences. The intention of this book is to help you see the detail that is the evidence of his dilemmas. Being armed with this information, you will not only see more, you will see earlier. Does your dog's emotional state affect how you feel?

Failing to read the signs

The early clues are all here: tense legs, head lowered, tight lips, looking away trying to avoid eye contact.

The Terrier escalates his behaviour when he is forced further into a situation he finds highly threatening. However, he still avoids aiming at the perceived threat.

- Does the look he gives you when he knows you are going out without him make you feel bad?
- Does his fear of the vet make you dread making an appointment?
- Do you find it difficult to stop him doing something because you know he's having fun?
- Does his excitement and *joie de vivre* take you there, too?

When you are with your dog, you are continually interpreting his emotional state. The aim of this book is to increase your awareness and deepen your understanding so that you can:

- Identify the detail of what you are seeing.
- Discover the cause of his emotions.
- Make changes so your dog's life is less stressful, and his relationship with you is even better.

If you work out the emotions your dog is experiencing and why it is triggering certain behaviours, you have a far greater chance of stepping in to help, support and, hopefully, resolve the situation. Sometimes it is your own behaviour that can have unintended consequences. You think you are doing the right thing by your dog – such as giving him hugs and kisses, or trying to make him be more sociable with other dogs – but this may be the very cause of his stress or anxiety.

He will be signaling what he is feeling, but if this goes unnoticed he will be forced to escalate his behaviour, going up a level to make his message clearer. This could have negative and even disastrous consequences. However, if you pick up on the clues, you will be able to change or moderate what you are doing. This will have a major impact on your dog's enjoyment of life, reduce his feelings of stress, avoid anxiety and improve his mental and physical wellbeing.

Chapter One

PLAYING DETECTIVE

Picking up emotional clues

If you have owned and loved a dog, you know beyond any shadow of doubt, that dogs are emotional beings. You know your dog has highs and lows on a daily basis; there are things he loves and situations he gets excited about. You know his favourite games, the person he greets most exuberantly, and the person he settles and relaxes with. You also know there are things he hates and situations that worry him – whether it's fireworks, going to the vet, watching you pack a suitcase or leaving him at home.

How do you know how your dog is feeling? You may not think you are an expert in canine communication but by watching your dog, day in, day out, you start to pick up the subtleties of his body language. You put this into a context, observe his behaviour, and you can then make a very good stab at guessing his emotional state. Sometimes the signals are blatant and unmistakable; the extremes of emotion, such as anger, frustration, fear, excitement, are easy to read. But you will also be able to pick up on tiny details which indicate a change of mood – signs of contentment and wellbeing, or a developing sense of concern or discomfort. These will become the cornerstone of understanding how your dog feels.

Body language is so much more than tails, hackles, ears, teeth, growling and barking. Other things to look for are the tiny facial clues, where the dog moves and the tension within his body. You will also be able to pinpoint the more long-term effects, such as what a dog does after a specific event and how his bodily biological functions are affected. Of course it's not a simple one plus one equals two equation, but gauging the limitations and complexities of these clues serves only to enhance your skill.

There are many emotional states your dog experiences throughout his life but if you recall a situation, and the body language used, you will start to build up a picture as to how he expresses his emotional state. Many of the signals and clues you observe will overlap from one emotion to another. Your dog may display a few of the clues, or many, he may be very clear to read or extremely subtle but, with practice, you will become expert at detecting the signals he is sending out.

THE EVIDENCE

The evidence for dogs as emotional beings is not just a matter of hearsay among anthropomorphic owners; there is measurable evidence in the form of escalating pulse rates and the levels of bio-chemicals and hormones that get pumped around the body. Recent research also shows the activation of different parts of the brain in response to a range of emotional sounds such as crying, growling, sighing or laughter. There are biological changes that lead to obvious bodily responses such as urination, defecation, and gland release, panting, paw sweating, sudden 'dandruff' appearance – all responses that may be witnessed in significantly frightening situations. But there are many other clues as to the dog's emotional state.

In the 1990s Turid Rugaas was at the forefront of presenting groundbreaking research on canine communication to the pet-owning public, which was gathered from watching thousands of hours of video footage. Rugaas recorded and analysed the body language and strategies that dogs use to reflect emotions and avoid conflict; she called these 'calming signals' as they had a calming effect on the other dog involved. These days we have sophisticated technology that makes spotting this often fleeting signaling even easier – 12 photos a second, 100 frames a second on video, plus access to footage on social media platforms – meaning that an increasing number of people can observe communication in slow motion and in astonishing detail.

The vast collection of behaviours, vocalisations and body language signals that help us to determine a dog's emotional state fit into five categories:

1. AUDIBLE INFORMATION

Dog lover or not, everyone recognises a bark, a whine, a snarl or the curious sound of a dog howling. Dog owners recognise not only their own dog's bark among other dogs, but also know that barking serves many functions – telling you there is a visitor, urging you to throw that toy, prompting you to open the door to the garden. You understand what your dog is 'saying', and you can also work out his mood, detecting if he is excited or anxious.

Barking has many uses; it is a form of greeting and is also used for expressing excitement, frustration and as a warning. But there are a lot of other sounds that dogs make that are used during interactions:

Howling is used when a fellow dog/person is missing. It can be eerily infectious in a gathering of dogs. Husky/Nordic type also use it as a form of greeting.

Whimpering is the sound made by a dog who is experiencing distress, fear or pain.

Whining is a higher-pitched sound made by dogs asking for, or wanting something.

Whistling is commonly heard among the German Shepherd population who use high-pitched whistling to express excitement or frustration. Whistling, which can take the form of a repetitive sequence of sigh-like endings, is also used by some dogs who are struggling to cope with being home alone.

Moaning sounds like a groan but with a hint of a grumbling growl. It is used by a dog under pressure when he has been disturbed or is wanting a dog companion to back off. There is no lip movement.

Growls come in a wide range of volume and level of ferocity, even from the same dog. It is a warning sign and will escalate until a dog resorts to warning air-snaps.

Heavy panting in the form of fast breathing, with a particularly noisy exhalation, is a play invitation.

Snort – a noisy exhalation though the nose – may also be used with a head dip as a play invite to another dog. It is almost, but not quite, a sneeze.

Cheek puffing is often used when greeting and it is almost inaudible. An excited dog will puff out his cheeks, without any related mouth or head movement.

Teeth chattering can be observed in some dogs when they are in a high anticipatory state; it is particularly related to food, toys or hunting.

Hissing is a sound which escapes through the dog's exposed teeth, and is mostly used as a form of greeting. However, a hissy snort, when air is passed through a wrinkled nose, can be an almost silent warning.

Snuffling, Snorting, Huffing is adopted by many of the short-nosed breeds, such as the Shih Tzu or the Pug, and generally used when greeting. Some dogs use a snorting or hissing snarl as a form of warning.

The absence of vocalisation can also be significant. For example, a deadly serious dog fight involves no communication. It may also indicate illness or a level of inhibition or shutting down.

Listen carefully and know what is normal for your dog... and enjoy listening out for all those often overlooked communicative, breathy sounds.

2. GROSS MOVEMENT

These are movements that can be mapped out on the ground. If we think of dogs meeting each other, the following actions are the mappable components:

- Approaching in a direct straight line.
- Taking a curved path around or towards each other.
- Spinning to avoid a rear end sniff.
- Moving around the other dog.
- Turning on the spot and going in the opposite direction.
- Stopping or moving backwards.

There is even more information to be gained when you analyse the speed of these behaviours, the extremes of fast and slow generally indicating high arousal. If play accelerates to top level, for example, it usually ends in tears.

CALMING SIGNALS

MEETING A NEW DOG

Some of the common calming signals used by dogs when unsure of each other on a first meeting.

Curving around – avoiding a direct approach.

A head turn away.

Avoiding eye contact.

Sniffing, so breaking direct contact.

Tongue flick/lip lick.

CAMERA SHY

Some of the same signals used by dogs when either unhappy about the staring camera, or not at ease with how they are or have been positioned.

A shake off.

Head turn and tongue flick.

Having a scratch.

Yawning.

Whole body turn away or tongue flick.

Blink and eye looking away.

3. BODY MOVEMENTS AND POSTURE

How is the dog holding his head – very upright, or forward with lowered neck, or down and turned away? What is he doing with his tail? Is it soft and wagging, tucked tightly under, rigid and vibrating? Is his back arched or relaxed, are his legs stiff or relaxed? An added significance to these body movements is muscle tension; stiff, rigid, tight muscles tell a different story to floppy, loose, soft muscles. Think of a dog that has rolled over when interacting with another dog. If he is fearful his body will be tense, his neck will be pushed into the ground, his legs will be held tightly into his body, his tail will be tucked between his legs and over his groin area. A dog that is rolling over as part of relaxed play will have floppy legs, his head and neck will move loosely, his tail will be flopped on the floor – everything will be soft, slow and casual.

We also need to observe where the dog's weight is being directed. Picture the dog who is frightened of a new rubbish bin – he stretches out his head and neck to smell it, but all his weight is at the rear, ready to retreat.

4. FACIAL EXPRESSIONS

A huge amount of information is displayed in facial expression, ranging from the obvious snarl to the more subtle signal where the corner of the lips are held back. It may be a fleeting blink or flick of the tongue up towards the nose, a brief yawn or a quick glance to see if the 'threat' is still evident. There are also many held movements, such as the furrowed brow, stares looking away or eyes held wide open or half closed. As humans we give many similar clues but we certainly don't have the amazing range of ear movements, or the ability to point our whiskers!

Like us, dogs are able to focus their senses, but their ability to individually orientate each ear makes this much more obvious. Under pressure, some dogs will also split where each eye is looking, giving very big clues as to what they are thinking about.

5. PHYSICAL REACTIONS

Emotional reactions can also be picked up from bodily responses which can be as obvious as submissive urination to the more subtle sign of damp paw prints on a vet's table where an anxious dog has sweated during an examination. It does not take a genius to work out that a sudden release of the anal glands, with its unmistakable fishy smell, or a dog that loses bowel control in this situation is showing signs of stress. Dogs also resort to displacement behaviours when they are expressing concern or conflict. These are based on natural behaviours such as panting, shaking or scratching – but the context gives vital clues:

Lip licking: A brief tongue flick up to the nose is a common sign of unease.

Panting which involves taking fast, shallow breaths, occurs when a dog is stressed or in pain. Conversely a dog will stop panting, and appear to hold his breath when, for example, he is concerned about an imminent interaction with another dog, or when faced with a procedure he finds threatening.

Yawning may be a sign of stress levels increasing. This could be when a dog is expecting something unpleasant or when he is being reprimanded. It is often seen when a dog is uncomfortable about something you are doing to him, or about to do to him. He is indicating that he is slightly uneasy with the procedure, whether it be handling him, clipping on his lead or even approaching him.

Sniffing can be used as an avoidance strategy. A dog who is trying to avoid confrontation with a boisterous exuberant playmate may become very focused on sniffing the bushes – almost as though he was pretending – in order to avoid potential contact.

His nose will be down but the eyes are the giveaway, checking out what is happening elsewhere. Your dog may also use sniffing as an avoidance strategy when he is interacting with you. For example, if during past recalls he has been reprimanded for being slow to return, he may attempt to calm you down by sniffing on his way back. If only he could realise how badly his attempts at placating misfire…

Rolling may be adopted by a dog experiencing stress or emotional conflict. Rolling over is a sign of submission when a younger or an anxious dog meets another dog. The submissive roll over is also seen when a dog is greeting people or if he feels threatened. Look out for the accompanying body language: his tail is tucked, there is tension in the neck and limbs, the eyes are wide and the lips are tight. If you move away, he will spring up, ready to re-prostrate himself.

A shake off is a reaction to a stressful situation.

You will often see a shake off when a dog has been put back on the floor after being picked up, after being examined, or after a stressful encounter with another dog.

Scratching may occur when a dog is stressed or appears to be confused. He will often use this strategy in a training situation as a means of buying time. It's as if he is saying: "I don't know what you want so I'll have a scratch while I think about it".

Shivering/trembling is a reaction to major stress. The toy breeds, though, are particularly prone to shivering when feeling both excited anticipation and concern at the same time. .

Toileting, particularly an urge to pass faeces, can accompany stressful experiences. Consequently, it will be more liquid or passed more frequently than usual. For other dogs, the opposite can be true; they need to be significantly relaxed before they can toilet. This reluctance is often observed with puppies on their first, highly stimulating walks. For adults novelty of place, or new dogs in the area, leads to an increase in urine marking and dramatic scratch-backs afterwards.

Extreme fear can lead to the involuntary passing of faeces, urine, and pungent smelling anal gland discharge.

Sweaty paws can be a telltale sign of unease. Dogs only sweat from their ears and their paws, so if you see damp footprints on the table following a veterinary examination, it is evidence of stress from a dog that has been restrained and, therefore, physically inactive.

Dandruff may be seen when brushing the coat, but an observable rising layer of snowy dandruff – old skin cells – demonstrates the physiological effect of stress.

TAILS – AN EMOTIONAL BAROMETER

How your dog holds his tail, and how he moves it, reveals specific facets of his character. But making a blanket assumption that a wagging tail is a sign of a happy dog, or a that a happy dog always wags his tail is too simplistic. You only have to visualise what a dog is doing with his tail when he is standing still to realise that breed type and conformation are highly influential. Some breeds and some individuals express a lot of emotion through the tension of the tail or the hold of the curl; others convey their feelings by how

much they wag their tail, and the speed of wagging.

Whether a dog has his tail clamped tightly over his backside, or loosely held, will give the biggest clue as to his emotional state. Tail position is, indeed, a great barometer for telling you how your dog feels, but your interpretation is governed by knowing how that breed, and that individual, uses their tail. Anyone who has owned a Dalmatian knows that the constantly wagging tail is not an indication of 'happiness' – but simply that he is awake! Likewise, the partially tucked under tail of the Greyhound does not suggest that he is desperately 'unhappy'; it is just his default tail position when nothing much is going on.

Tail wagging is frequently observed in situations of emotional conflict where the dog is feeling both excited and worried. Three-week-old puppies competing with their littermates for the best teat to suckle, will wag furiously. A young dog greeting an older dog, or an adult dog encountering an unknown or frightening dog, may show a lot of appeasement along with a tail that is held tightly over the backside, with the lower portion in a fast wag. The clamped tail tells us a lot.

Instinctively a dog uses his tail to protect his anus and genitals so when it is clamped tightly over his backside, he is clearly feeling threatened. The dog who feels the need to appease a person will wag only the lower part of his tail, evidencing the emotional conflict he is experiencing. Delighted to see you – yes – but also worried enough to seek your approval. How does your dog hold his tail when he greets you?

INTERPRETING THE CLUES

TELLING TAILS	POMERANIAN SPITZ POODLE	GREYHOUND RHODESIAN RIDGEBACK	BOXER DALMATIAN	LABRADOR GOLDEN RETRIEVER
ABOUT TO GO FOR A WALK				
EXPLORING AND INVESTIGATING ON A WALK				
BORED OR ABOUT TO SETTLE DOWN				
STARTLED BY NOVEL NOISE				

Dogs are not as uniform in shape as humans; the short-coated, prick-eared, tightly curled tailed Basenji looks very different to the long-coated, loose-tailed Cavalier King Charles Spaniel. Bear in mind that:

- Some dogs, such as Spaniels with their long, immobile ears, will be physically unable to give some clues.
- Some dogs will be groomed (e.g. a Miniature Schnauzer presented for the show ring) or physically altered (dogs with docked tails), making some clues impossible to detect.
- Some dogs will be presenting these clues but due to structure/coat/skin, the clues are in a reduced form.

The dictates of a breed, or the way it is presented for the show ring, can make facial expressions hard to read.

This is true of a dog with no coat, such as the Mexican Hairless, a dog with a long coat such as the Old English Sheepdog, or a dog with wrinkly, furrowed skin, such as Shar Pei.

It is the body language and behaviours used when a dog is experiencing obvious and extreme emotions that forms the basis of much of our interpretation, but it is the progression towards the more exaggerated and obvious body language that is most revealing. So, for example, if your dog is very frightened of lightning he might learn to pick up an early clue that this may occur, a clue that we might not even be aware of, such as the change in atmospheric ionisation, and so he starts watching and following you. His ears might be low, his eyes slightly wide with whiskers held close, his mouth will be held closed and his stance and body muscles won't be relaxed and soft, but he is still aware of you and will respond, albeit in a slightly distracted fashion.

When the thunder starts to rumble, you get another set of clues: pacing around, trying to get in closer contact with you or checking for possible dens. His ears will be held tightly back, his eyes are wide, his lips tight, and his head and neck are lowered. The physiological clues will also start to appear: panting, trembling, pupils dilated, an easily felt increase in heartbeats, and treats become unpalatable. He struggles to concentrate or do things you ask of him. The lightning crack leads to extreme body language, so much so that nobody – even a 'non doggy' person – is left in any doubt as to how he is feeling. But if you can pick up on the early, subtle signals, you will know how your dog is feeling at a much earlier stage and will be able to intervene and help.

As you become proficient, you will detect minute changes. Your dog thinks he hears a crack of lightening in the distance and he stills, his head drops, his neck and face tense, he does a lick towards his nose, he blinks his eyes, he moves about for a while, taking longer to settle down than normal. Teasing out these small changes in body language, muscle tension and the ability to recover may be details, but the information they provide is huge.

Another area that informs our interpretation is the history of an individual dog. Let us look at the histories of three dogs, now 12 months of age, detailing how their behaviour has evolved:

NOW	AS PUPPIES
Bark at strangers in the street.	Froze or tried to back away.
Give a dramatic, aggressive display if another dog tries to sniff them.	Rolled over or, in a desperate cringing fashion, tried to lick and appease the other dog.
Bite their owner if held by the collar.	Acted the clown, turning it into a game or wriggling around.

These extreme behaviours nearly always started out as something that appeared to be of no consequence. But these early reactions can prove to be highly revealing and hold the key to interpreting the dog's current behaviour. Again, early detection is key to taking action and preventing problems developing.

Much of the obvious or extreme body language you see in your dog can also be observed as a less exaggerated form, so we get:

- A look away or head turn, rather than moving away.
- The head lowered rather than a full body drop.
- A head bob rather than a full play bow.
- A nose or a muzzle bump rather than a play (or otherwise) bite.
- A silent bark used as a play invite rather than a loud, demanding bark.

Knowing the exaggerated form helps you to spot and understand the intention in the less exaggerated clues.

DEGREES OF RELAXATION

Relaxed

- On waking after a night's sleep – calm and easily goes back to sleep.
- Positioned for snoozing casual, not ready for action.
- Lying with back to potential source of action or not positioned to watch.
- Soft muscle tension throughout body.
- Tail, eyes, ears in soft held position.
- Responds calmly or not at all to interruptions.
- May move an ear or eyes, but not head.

Trying to settle

- Cave/den seeking.
- In resting place circles, digs or scratches.
- Often with different rituals for a nap or an overnight settle.
- Repeatedly getting up or down.
- Moans, groans or sighs as lying down.
- Self-grooming, repetitive licking or suckling behaviour.

Settled, not relaxed

- Reacts to low level stimuli. Follows movements with eyes, ears or whole head.
- Frequent repositioning.
- Sphinx position – chin on, or between, front legs.
- Lying with head positioned for seeing.
- Blinks or head nods as tries to stay awake.
- Eyes may close but easily disturbed.
- Stiff legs.

DEGREES OF EXCITEMENT

Happy, relaxed enjoyment

- Calm, slow movements asking for more.
- Eyes soft, eyelids may partially close.
- Facial muscles and skin relaxed – no tension wrinkles.
- Lips and ears held softly.
- Soft body muscle tension.
- Tail is up or out, slow wag.

Excited

- Can't stay still, lots of movement.
- Fast movement.
- Jumping up, front feet bounce.
- Undulating, body-led fast tail wag.
- Spinning, barking.
- Eyes and ears focused.
- Tense muscles, pant, break wind, burp and drool.

Extreme excitement

- Vocalisation – high-pitched, repetitive and out of control.
- Lots of movement – maybe pointless and repetitive.
- Intense and fast responses.
- Reduced tolerance to interference.
- Working behaviours of the breed evident.
- Fully alert ears.
- Dark eyes.
- Urination, defecation.

DEGREES OF CONCERN

A little worried/uncomfortable/not settled

- Faffing behaviours: mad runaround.
- Invokes chasing games, over-the-top behaviour, jumping and rolling around
- Behaviour isn't always directed at cause.
- Lip licks, yawn, blink, scratch, brief gulps, snorts.
- Sniffing elsewhere, glancing away, curving around.
- Difficulty focusing, concentrating consistently slow response to commands or requests.

Concerned or distressed in a situation

- Can't settle. Appears to settle but actually inhibited.
- Repetitive behaviours.
- Seeks a comfort object.
- Dark eyes.
- Lip lick, yawn, head turn away.
- Avoiding – takes wide berth.
- Can't eat treats. Snatches at treats.
- Panting, pacing.
- Toileting patterns not normal.
- May not be fully aware of you.
- Either can't slow, or do known commands/tricks.
- Tense, stiff body.

DEGREES OF FEAR

Frightened

- Try to escape/den.
- Back off.
- Try to repel/see off/get rid of.
- Momentary freezes.
- Lowered body/ head.
- Tense body.
- Weight balances away from...
- On tip toes.
- Pant/drool, hair drop/dandruff.
- Toileting.
- May hardly be aware of you.
- Unable to respond to any requests.

Extreme or sudden fear

- Escape attempts regardless of pain or safety and despite barriers, e.g. doors, crate, on lead or being held.
- Drop to ground, freeze, curl into a ball, shut down.
- Involuntary urination or defecation, vomit, anal gland release.
- Pant, tremble, wide eyes, tight lips, tense stiff body, dark eyes.
- Urination, defecation.

BEFORE AND AFTER

The level of emotional impact a dog is experiencing can also be gleaned from looking at the changes in body language that occur before and after an incident, such as your departure from home and your subsequent return. The dog that 'hardly notices' you getting ready to leave and, on your return greets you, but soon gets on with his normal behaviours will not be stressed in your absence. He is aware that you are preparing to leave – changing shoes, collecting keys, etc. – and he may show a subtle change in facial expression or choose to go and settle on his bed, but he is not unduly concerned. But for dogs, this is an emotionally difficult time, which becomes increasingly severe as he picks up the clues of your impending absence earlier.

Your dog's body language after the event is a big clue as to the impact of a situation. This can range from transient clues, such as a body shake off or stopping to urinate after a slightly tense meeting with another dog, to the prolonged and highly effusive greeting of a dog who is stressed when left alone at home. This process of recovery – as he is returning to 'normal' behaviour – is a useful measure of the dog's emotional arousal. So the excessive greeting given by an anxious dog on his owner's return will lessen in time and intensity as he makes progress in his retraining programme. A burst of activity after an incident may also be indicative of emotional stress and, again, will reduce as the dog grows in confidence. Though often overlooked, this is a big clue that the situation was too difficult for your dog.

The dog that goes wild on returning from a difficult walk, or behaves worse after being reprimanded is getting rid of pent up stress. This type of relief behaviour may also be seen after a dog has coped with a situation he finds difficult. He puts up with being petted by a stranger and when it is over he has a sudden burst of activity – a single jump up on his owner, a body shake off, a quick spin, or a momentary play invite and a dash that quickly evaporates. These after-behaviours occur when there would be measurable physiological changes happening during the event, such as heightened breathing/heart rate, or cortisol and adrenaline increases – all due to increased arousal.

Following a stressful situation, relief can take the form of a high-energy outburst.

The hunched back, lowered neck and tight tail shows this dog is unhappy about being picked up and manages to avoid it by escaping...

...This leads to a giddy dash – although the nearside ear is still very owner-focused.

The tucked tail and tightly pulled back lips are the gesture of a worried dog – not a request for a tummy rub...

...The relief when the interaction ceases is demonstrated with a shake (see lead) and a bounce up on his owner.

This amazing sequence of photos clearly illustrate the emotional conflict this Jack Russell is experiencing. He is clearly confused – both scared and excited – by his male owner (see photos on page 8). He tries to act the clown in an attempt to divert what he perceives as a potential threat (see page 54).

Although the eyes, ears and head set look as if he is trying to invite play, his weight is backwards. This, along with the following photos, confirm that his strategy is to avoid contact.

He obeys and rolls over but in the opposite direction than that requested – to be further away. His neck and legs are tense and trying to keep the owner at a distance.

As soon as the owner moves his hand away, the Jack Russell does a sudden leap up and is about to do a crazy, seemingly playful, dash around.

ACCUMULATIVE EFFECT

Just like us, dogs are affected by the build up, over time, of difficult events. While each of these events may seem trivial, in isolation, if they occur so frequently that stress levels do not diminish and the dog is unable to return to a state of rest and relaxation in-between, it eventually leads to a crisis. We humans find it perfectly understandable that a series of minor irritations can lead to a major outburst. For us – and for a dog – it is a case of going one step too far. We are also prone to being tipped over the edge by something that does not directly relate to our source of irritation. With dogs this might lead us to describe an outburst as being sudden or unpredictable. In fact, the better we become at discerning subtle indications of stress and unease, the more an outburst becomes predictable and therefore avoidable.

LONG-TERM OVER-AROUSAL AND LONG-TERM ANXIETY

The long-term nature of these conditions means that we are mostly noting clues from patterns of behaviour rather than specific momentary body language clues. These clues are evident when the cause of the triggers is arousal, or the source of anxiety, is not occurring at that particular time. So if your dog is constantly chasing the family cat, he will display signs of long-term over-arousal even while holidaying at your friend's house for the weekend. They are the symptoms of being over stimulated on a daily basis; they have led to changes in the brain and nervous system that may take weeks or even months to reduce.

However, the good news is that by creating the right conditions, arousal levels can be lowered, making it feasible to change even the most ingrained behaviour patterns. It is frequent exposure to anxiety-inducing experiences that build up over time producing long-term anxiety which, in turn, leads to physiological changes. Again, the anxiety-inducing situation – crossing a busy road, for example – may only happen twice a day. But if the dog is anxious there will be evidence even when he is in the safety of his own home. Sometimes this can mean that significant detective work is needed to determine the original fear, which is the cause of the long-term anxiety.

LONG-TERM ANXIETY

Anxiety builds up over a period of time and a dog may show some, or all, of the reactions listed below:

Reaction to you

- Training, learning hindered.
- Lowered tolerance.
- Touch sensitive.
- Needy behaviours: can't relax, won't leave your side, follows you everywhere.

Reaction to the environment

- Hyper-vigilant – always on the lookout.
- Over sensitive to sound, novelty, changes.
- Exploratory behaviours reduced.
- Repetitive behaviours – tail chasing, shadow chasing, pacing.
- Self-comforting behaviours.
- Excessive self-grooming – anal/genital licking, scratching, lick granulas commonly develop on the wrists.

Sleep and rest

- Restless, always on the go.
- Sleeping too much, or not enough.
- Difficulty settling.
- Some degrees of pacing.
- May have a permanently tired (stressed) looking face.

Physiological responses

- On/off food.
- Harder to keep weight on.
- Disruptions in toileting behaviour.
- Urine marking in the house.
- Susceptible to illness and disease.
- Loose bowels/constipation/flatulence.
- Skin and coat problems.

CONFLICTING EMOTIONS

There are times when a dog displays emotions which seem to be at odds with each other. He may be settled, but not relaxed – something novel is happening in the house, for example – and so he will keep resettling himself. He may be excited, but worried – greeting a stranger, for example – and show a mixture of appeasing and over-the-top behaviour. These are the mild outcomes of conflicting emotional states.

Extreme behaviours may be seen when walking past some of the 'problem' dogs in rescue centres. A dog may be excited but frustrated – barking, scratching, pulling at the barrier, spinning, circling or doing enormous leaps. He may be frustrated but fearful, in which case he might bark or bounce on his back legs, mostly towards the back of his pen. He may shake his bedding or his toys, again at the back of the pen, or may alternate between the front and back. It is these conflicting emotions that are often deeper in impact leading to stronger and more undesirable responses.

Every day our dogs greet us, go for walks, have playtimes and settle down with us. We presume they are totally positive experiences for our dogs. The dog elects to engage in these activities and appears to enjoy them. However, under closer inspection of his body language and behaviour, it may become evident that he wouldn't rate these as five-star experiences. This is important feedback that informs us where we can improve out services!

DO DOGS TELL LIES?

We cannot possibly leave a discussion on clues/signals and body language without addressing what is going on with the dog who is good as gold in situations where you were expecting problems. The dog's behaviour appears exemplary – he shows none of the silly or aggressive behaviours that you would have confidently predicted – yet you cannot ask for the 'good' behaviour to order. For example:

The dog is 'good' when other people handle/ examine him – the vet, groomer, dog trainer – but he won't even stay still if you try to examine him.

The dog is 'good' in one context, but reacts badly in another apparently similar situation. When he is in town he walks quietly, taking no notice of the people he passes, but when he goes on his routine neighbourhood walk he barks the moment he sees someone.

The dog is fine with people or dogs he meets away from home, but he will not tolerate the same person/dog in his house.

These apparently incongruent behaviours make the 'good' behaviour appear even more dazzling. But, in fact, it is much more a case of the dog putting up with an undesirable situation, which you can tell by picking up the clues of his true emotional state. The dog is not being 'good' he is simply inhibiting his behaviour. He has found a recipe for survival. So yes, the dog is good as gold - he is certainly behaving much more acceptably. But don't kid yourself that he is happy or fine – he is not. The body language he is using is that of a frightened dog. He is not brave enough to even risk running away, and he is too worried to use defensive behaviour. But when he is with you, or at home, he feels more confident and will employ these tactics.

The proof that he has inhibited his behaviour can be seen as soon as the situation changes and he no longer needs to be 'good'. His relief will be palpable, shown by a body shake off, a quick jump up at, or off you, or a few silly seconds, doing something daft and fast. He might suddenly have a huge desire to scratch, even though he's not itchy, or he may rush off to relieve himself and do an impressive scratch back. A "good boy" – yes. A nice experience for him – no. Big and small clues tell us otherwise, but if you have already felt these are situations that he "puts up with", then you have interpreted his emotional state. Now you can look closer to see the many clues that confirm your interpretation.

This inhibited 'good' behaviour is undeniably useful, but regularly subjecting a dog to this level of fear is abusive. We should only allow it to happen in situations of necessity rather than convenience. Lying? He's not lying, he's trying his best.

We love our dogs because they allow us to share their emotions. The more skilled we become at reading their body language, the better able we are to make informed decisions that will enhance their quality of life.

Dogs can find the human race unpredictable and frightening; some certainly think we are quick to show aggression and use threatening techniques. This may

In a difficult situation, resignation or shutting down may be the only option.

The German Shepherd is only thinking of his ball, but the Pug perceives a threat so freezes with his neck pushed into the snow; his contracted back legs and front left paw try to keep the Shepherd away. The way he is holding his head and tail tell us he is familiar with the Shepherd.

With a distant stare, ears back and neck lowered, this dog freezes and resigns himself to whatever is his fate.

With tail tucked and tense spread toes, this Dachshund wants to be where he's looking, not where he is.

have been totally unintentional as far as the human was concerned, but we have to see things from the dog's perspective. It is only by addressing what the dog perceives that we can change his emotional perception and build his confidence. If this is too hard, taking too long, or is not practical for you or him, get professional assistance from someone who will work on helping you build his confidence, working on his underlying emotional state and not simply focusing on his symptomatic behaviours.

SUMMING UP

A range of emotional states can be determined through observing your dog's body language and behaviour. The clues are in the form of:

- The sounds he makes.
- Where he moves.
- How he moves – particularly muscle tension.
- Facial expressions.
- Bodily responses.

Interpretation will be influenced by:

- Physical breed characteristics.
- Knowing your own dog's normal body language.
- Understanding dog behaviour.
- His history.
- The context.

Apparently unpredictable outbursts are usually due to smaller stresses building up. Long-term anxiety and long-term over-arousal will be in evidence even when the dog is away from the source. Being worried can lead to inhibited behaviour. This can make the dog appear 'good' when he is under pressure.

With tightly tucked tail this little Chihuahua has gone still not to be good, but because he is very frightened of the mouse. Despite the temptation, he faces away to avoid looking at it. He probably fears he might provoke it!

Chapter Two

JOINING THE FAMILY CIRCLE

Finding a place in your home

The reactions of a puppy or a new dog when he first comes home need to be closely observed as they will inform the way you guide him and help him to deal with new situations. Obviously, there are many influences at work which will affect the way he behaves including breed/breed type, genetic make-up, inherited temperament and early rearing experiences.

These are the influences that have been at work before you brought your puppy home and, in the case of a rescued dog, there will be a significant amount of history – known and unknown – to take on board. But the common starting point is that you cannot change what has gone before – you are now the major influence in your dog's life and you can decide what experiences he should be exposed to.

You need to read the signals your dog is sending out so you can provide the support and guidance he needs. For the purposes of this chapter, we will look at five types of reaction:

1. The confident puppy
2. The less confident puppy
3. The overwhelmed puppy
4. The appeasing puppy
5. The excitement-seeking puppy

It is important to bear in mind that a puppy, or a new dog, may well fall into one category in a situation he finds difficult or stressful, but his reactions may be entirely straightforward in another situation when he does not perceive a threat. It is for this reason that you need to observe your puppy closely so you know what state he is in, and can respond in the appropriate manner.

A puppy may show concern when confronted with a new situation or experience, but it is the time he takes to recover that is critical.

1. THE CONFIDENT PUPPY

Exploring his new home
Within a few minutes of arriving home you will see the character of your puppy begin to emerge as he explores his surroundings. If a pup has been taken to different places by the breeder, or he is genetically hard-wired to be confident, he will be happy striking out on his own and getting to grips with his new home.

With ears up and pointing forwards his exploring will be spontaneous and wide-ranging. As he investigates his body posture will be upwards and forwards with no muscle tension. Lots will delight him and little surprise him. If he happens to be startled his reaction will be short lived – he will immediately approach what surprised him again. Perhaps tentatively, initially, but within a second or two he will return to his previous confident posture and continue exploring.

Meeting the family

The confident puppy wants to play almost immediately. Now he is separated from his mother and his littermates, his new human family members will become the substitutes for play and interaction.

He may not appreciate being picked up and cuddled, but he will respond as if nothing much is happening – continuing to try and play with whatever is near his mouth. The play will be soft with no sudden or fast movements of resistance or concern. If he is tired, or play-satiated, he will settle into the nearest lap.

2.   THE LESS CONFIDENT PUPPY

Exploring his new home

A less confident pup that has had limited experiences will be a lot more cautious. He will be torn between going forward to investigate and hanging back and staying closer to you – as you have now become his major point of security. As you walk, you will find yourself tripping over him, as he tries to keep within your range.

He will take a few minutes to pluck up the courage to explore and he will, initially, focus on one area, broadening his range as he feels more confident. He often needs time to acclimatise and may need to be exposed to an environment more than once to feel comfortable. For example, he may be very tentative exploring the garden the first time, but the next time he goes out there he will be much more confident.

While the confident puppy recovers almost immediately from something that startles him, this

... AND ON THE FIRST DAY ...

Helping Out

A puppy's initial reactions to his home and family are highly informative. To a greater or lesser extent, they will indicate how he is likely to react to new environments and when meeting new people.

If you orchestrate these early home experiences to be easy for him – and observe him closely – you can plan on-going experiences accordingly, thus providing a solid foundation for your puppy's on-going education.

puppy will take a few breaths before he carefully moves off and resumes exploring as previously. If he keeps being startled, he will become increasingly sensitised.

Meeting the family

The less confident puppy will hold himself back when he is greeting or interacting. It is not complete avoidance, but it is a reluctance, particularly if the person is reaching out or trying to touch him.

The less confident pup wants to meet and greet, but he struggles. When touched or handled, he will probably stay in place, but he will have a low body posture and will often back off. He may do a partial or momentary freeze, but this is more likely to be seen as a dipping of the body. In some cases, this could progress to a growl or an air-snap if the puppy is really failing to find the space he feels he needs.

As a puppy settles into his new home, he will appear increasingly relaxed and confident but in novel situations, or with new people, you may observe the old reaction. If this occurs, don't be afraid to slow down such experiences.

3.   THE OVERWHELMED PUPPY

Exploring his new home

The instinct to chase anything that moves is very strong in most puppies, but the overwhelmed pup will not only show limited desire to explore, he will also resist this urge. Whether walking, trotting or running, he will move in a stilted, controlled fashion with a low body posture. Exploration will be tentative, typically carried out with ears down, and stretching his neck and head forwards to investigate. He will keep his weight backwards in preparation for a retreat. He may start moving around with a normal posture within half-an-hour or so, but it could take a few days.

The overwhelmed puppy shows a preference for den-like areas, so it is important to provide a safe haven – a base where he feels safe and secure. He may then spend a significant amount of time being quite still and observing from his safe place, but mental exhaustion will mean that he sleeps a lot.

Explorations will start from this safe place, and each time he ventures out he will grow in stature and explore further and further afield. However, he will be easily startled by seemingly insignificant events – a sudden noise or movement and he will bolt back to the safety of his den. Alternatively, he may crouch down for five seconds or more and then do a stilted retreat.

Meeting the family

Instinctively, you may feel you want to encourage the overwhelmed puppy from his place of refuge, luring him with treats or picking him up to cuddle him. Your aim is to give reassurance, but there is a danger that he will quickly build up a bad association with people – and with treats. Hard though it may be, this puppy needs the time and space to make up his own mind.

The overwhelmed puppy should only be given attention when he voluntarily emerges from his refuge, and even this should be done very subtly. Position yourself so you are sitting with your back to him. If he starts to investigate you, or the area near you, don't immediately pounce on him, or startle him with lots of praise. React quietly and calmly and give him the time and space to seek you out.

If approached, the overwhelmed puppy will back off, or he may even try to hide. If he is cornered, picked up or held, he may completely freeze, or go into a panic struggle as he tries to get away. He may give a greeting, but it will be very much on the lines of small advances and retreats. However, if he receives minimal attention, and therefore feels under minimal pressure – and his retreats give him a feeling of safety – he will gradually retreat less and less.

The overwhelmed puppy requires very little pro-active engagement; your behaviour should remain as neutral as possible. It is better to keep meetings to one person at a time to give him a chance to learn, without being even more overwhelmed by the experience. Physical contact – stroking, holding and, particularly restraining – should be built up very slowly.

You will need to observe his body language at all times, and make efforts to avoid any interactions where he is trying to back off or is starting to go into freeze mode. If these interactions become too pressurised, he may resort to using aggressive displays to try to keep you at bay, or he may opt out, becoming passive or shutting down. Both the overwhelmed, and the less confident puppy, need to learn that people are safe and predictable. The overwhelmed puppy, in

PLUCKING UP THE COURAGE...

Following a short spell on a lap, but without being cuddled, our little Chihuahua (see page 7) still needs to assess the situation from a safe place. Her upright head and forward focus tells us she is nearly ready to investigate, but the partial hide and wrinkled face let us know she is not quite ready.

With feet planted and stretching forward, this puppy's desire for the treat is pushing him beyond his emotional comfort zone. He will gain confidence more quickly if he is allowed to proceed at his own pace.

particular, needs to be confident in the knowledge that he can decide when to approach people, and will not be approached by them. Retreating should always be a safe and available option.

4. THE APPEASING PUPPY

Meeting the family

The behaviour of an appeasing puppy is directly related to his interactions with people, which, initially means his new family. The behaviours an appeasing puppy displays are strongly related to how humans interact with him. His new family will have a significant influence.

Just like the overwhelmed puppy, the puppy that is showing appeasing behaviour also needs non-intervention to relieve the pressure he is feeling. He may keep offering tightly tucked sits, but instead of crowding in on him to praise him and fuss him, we need to back off and give him some space. This gives him the relief he needs so he won't resort to submissive displays or even submissive urination.

These automatic sits are offered when he is getting fussed and petted. His ears will be close to his head and pinned back, you will also see high-energy wriggling with the hindquarters lowered or dipped. He may repeatedly jump up and down, or offer repeated roll-overs. He will also be very licky when he is interacting with people and may push his body or head into them.

When the sit is offered, it will be very tense; he will hold his head very upright and may then roll over on to his back. Tempting though it may be to rub his tummy, it is not what he actually wants. By rubbing his tummy, his appeasing behaviours are very likely to increase. For this puppy – and in this situation – you should back away and interact calmly only when he is on his feet.

Even as he becomes familiar with the family you may see submissive urination. The appeasing puppy will produce a few drops of urine, or a small puddle, during greeting times. This is a sure sign that he needs more space and calmer interactions. In more extreme cases, he may even deposit faeces.

As this puppy becomes more settled, he will become increasingly bold and confident in situations he knows and with people he has learnt to trust. With new people, a combination of excitement and worry may refuel his need to appease. If this happens, you need to react very calmly and gently, as reprimands, or giving him a big fuss, will lead to further appeasement.

5. THE EXCITEMENT-SEEKING PUPPY

Exploring his new home

All puppies should show a degree of excitement as they explore a new environment. However, they have a limited attention span and will flit from one new thing to the next, investigating anything that moves, smells, or looks interesting. This reaction will be more extreme in an excitable puppy, but it is generally people and other animals that he finds most stimulating and completely irresistible.

Meeting the family

All young puppies will mouth and play-bite, but the over-excitable puppy will adopt a policy of dash in and grab. Sometimes a puppy may be interacting reasonably calmly but when the pressure increases – for example, a child comes into the equation or he is mildly reprimanded – his behaviour quickly escalates and he loses self-control. This is prompted by nervousness, worry, and often fatigue, and he finds a release in over-the-top behaviour. A human's high-pitched 'yip' or 'ouch' stops most puppies from hard biting – but for the excitable puppy it leads to faster and harder biting.

The excitement-seeking puppy quickly learns that it is the items that are not his toys that bring on a highly exciting game of chase. All he has to do is look towards you – and then sprint away – and it's game on!

Attempts at stopping unwanted behaviour by physically intervening, or giving verbal correction, serve only to increase them. If he is severely reprimanded, he will stop what he is doing and go still. He will lower his shoulders and neck and/or turn his head away. His ears will be pinned back. The body language he is displaying is that of fear. Guilt or apology are not within a puppy's emotional intelligence.

The outcome of such a response often leads to defensive aggression or play with aggressive overtones. This is frequently directed towards children who are unable to create this same level of fear as an adult when reprimanding. This is an unnecessary and undesirable situation for all concerned.

EDUCATION BEFORE EXPECTATION

A puppy arrives in your home having little or no idea of what behaviours humans find unacceptable or undesirable; it is your job to help him make the right choices. Develop your puppy's love of toys, chews, food activity and appropriate rubbish items (the inner tube of a toilet roll or a plastic bottle without the top) if you want him to choose them in preference to the other temptations which are all around him. If you attempt to use correction and reprimands to guide him in the right direction, you will become stressed and you risk your puppy become fearful.

INTERACTIONS WITH CHILDREN

Introducing a puppy, or a new dog, to children requires lots of management both of children and the puppy/dog. This will be particularly relevant for the less confident or excitable puppy, and will be vital if the overwhelmed puppy is to make any progress. Supervise and observe how the puppy is reacting.

The way children move, and the noises they make, are considerably less predictable than they way adults behave. Equally a child's reaction to a puppy will also vary for reasons the puppy will not understand. For a puppy, it is easy to misinterpret a scared child running away as an invitation to play.

Puppies can find children very difficult which is often shown by an acute need to know the child's whereabouts. Frequent looking to check where they are, or more severely a whole head movement; backing away or ducking is not conducive to a safe child-dog relationship. The use of gates and barriers will help to give everyone their own space.

PLAY-BITING

From a puppy's point of view, mouthing and biting is communication. It is what a puppy does with his littermates to initiate play and what he does to his mother to provoke a reaction. He is using his mouth all the time as a means of communicating and as a means of investigating. Fingers and toes are an endless source of fascination, the movement of arms and legs are irresistible, and a face held close is asking to be licked, or nipped if the puppy is over-excited. This is a completely natural extension of the behaviour he used with his littermates; it is simply transferred to nipping at shoes or trousers, chasing and ambushing you, or trying to hang on to a bit of clothing as you try to get away. To inhibit this type of behaviour – and avoid negative outcomes – you need to redirect his play-biting activity to toys (see Play-biting survival guide, page 28).

WHEN PLAY-BITING MISFIRES

For the puppy, play-biting is his principle means of communicating and if you put a dramatic stop to it, the puppy has not only lost his way of interacting, he may well become worried or frightened when dealing

with people. In a worst case scenario, this can develop into defensive biting when he feels under pressure, such as when he is being told off, restrained or moved from one place to another.

Biting and mouthing can also be the result of frustration – the puppy is being denied something and

This puppy's early biting experience was dealt with in a way that frightened her and caused her to lose trust in her owners. However, she is still desperate to play and interact. Note she is pulling downwards not backwards so she can own the toy. Observe where neck, shoulder and bodyweight are directed. The tail-set, ears held back, wide eyes and tight upper lip tell us she is on the verge of escalating to an aggressive display.

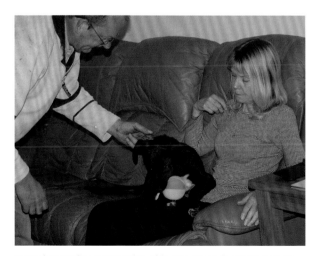

From her canine perspective, this youngster doesn't want to defend herself aggressively. She freezes, with wide, scared eyes, and avoids making eye contact, but still feels she should own the toy. Her expectation of a threat is confirmed as her owner takes hold of her collar.

28

he lashes out. This can be a straightforward case of redirection: you restrain your puppy when he wants to interact with someone, or do something, and the biting/mouthing is directed on to you. If unresolved, the puppy may increasingly resort to redirection. He will be quick moving, repeatedly turning round to nip, whereas genuine play biting is softer and slower.

THE IMPORTANCE OF SLEEP

A puppy needs a huge amount of sleep – and this does not just mean at night. Not only is your puppy growing at a rapid rate, he is mentally exhausting himself as he adapts to his new life. It may seem that a pup has so much energy that he can play forever, but down times are equally, if not more important, than playtimes. Rather like a toddler, an over-tired puppy becomes fractious and is much more likely to growl or nip.

He may become withdrawn as he can no longer cope with the pressure of interacting with his human family, or he may become hyped up and hysterical because he is too tired to think straight. A puppy that has sufficient rest will be active, inquisitive and ready to learn in his waking periods. A puppy that never gets unbroken periods of sleep during the day will become increasingly unpredictable and unreliable in his behaviour. He can appear wild and hyperactive.

Just as with children, a 'preparing to settle' routine can help a busy puppy to wind down so that he is able to rest.

Progress in the following stages:

1. Stimulation, which could be in the form of a walk or a play session.
2. Toileting and drink with minimal interaction.
3. Chew/lick toy in crate/playpen or quiet area, with no interaction.

Avoid future problems:

Do not leave your puppy to cry, whine or howl for prolonged periods:

- If he is making a fuss for only 5-10 minutes, he will get over it.
- If it is for longer than this he will need help so he learns, gradually, to cope on his own.

PLAY-BITING SURVIVAL GUIDE

The average 'normal' puppy wants to play nearly all the time he is awake, so get him hooked on toys.

You have seen how much he wants to chase and tug, so provide these games, making sure toys are much more interesting than your hands, hair, shoes, etc.

While playing, keep toys on the floor so as not to provoke jumping and snatching. Children need a line on toys so they can drag them around, keeping biting and grabbing directed downwards and on the toy.

Puppies are not developmentally ready for petting and cuddling unless they are sleepy. Attention of this kind will be viewed as play, which involves mouthing and biting. Don't try to fight this; wait until your puppy is a little older and is ready to enjoy tactile contact.

Be prepared to channel your puppy's behaviour before he mouths/play-bites. The more a behaviour is repeated, the more it becomes ingrained.

Use treats to help your puppy focus on something else when you are likely to trigger play-biting, e.g. when you are attaching a lead, putting on a harness, grooming or toweling him dry.

MEETING THE FAMILY DOG

Many households have more than one dog but introducing a new puppy to the resident dog isn't always immediately successful. So what does it say about our domesticated dogs if they are struggling with this interaction?

If you have a puppy that has been exposed to a number of adult dogs, or an adult that is accustomed to meeting puppies, you can pretty much assume that any introductions will pass off without complications and without the need for intervention. However, many adult dogs have very limited exposure to puppies and, by the nature of their age, a new puppy coming into a home has had limited exposure to adult dogs. The adult dog may feel petrified of this strange creature, which could lead to avoidance or proactive warnings; others will respond with play behaviours more appropriate for an adult dog.

An overly biddable dog, or a dog that is afraid to correct a puppy may be plagued and tormented to an unreasonable degree. On that very first encounter, an excitable puppy will do lots of appeasing behaviours –licking at the adult's mouth and squirming around. Naggingly, he will keep seeking approval from the adult. A more confident puppy may have a different approach, for example dive-bombing, grabbing and pulling the adult dog. A fearful puppy will flatten and roll over; he will try to keep his distance from the adult. All these reactions reflect a high level of arousal – it is very unusual for a new puppy to be blasé about an encounter with a new canine.

WHO WOULD YOU PUT ON LEAD? FIRST IMPRESSIONS

When introducing a puppy, or a new dog, to an existing family dog, we are often encouraged to adopt a "let them be" attitude in the belief that they are better left to work things out for themselves.

They will eventually reach an accommodation with each other and most encounters are comfortable after the first few days. Even in the worst cases, it will only be a month or so before the two find a way to

↑
The speed and heavy paw movement of this adult is too much for the puppy, who drops his head and reverses out of the situation. However, his tail carriage suggests he would like to be involved. If the adult was held on a lead, the pup could retreat, and re-engage, as he would feel safe.

With neck drawn up and back, and fairly tight lips, the adult Golden Retriever isn't quite as keen as the pup. You would need to be very observant with these two as some adults lack the confidence to tell a puppy to go away. Their relationship might progress more smoothly if the pup was kept on a lead and encounters kept brief. →

↑
The older dog is showing caution, twisting his neck outwards and avoiding the pup, but his gaze and face is focused on the pup. His ears and neck are held up so he is avoiding contact. In fact, he is more likely to jump away. The puppy is also wary, using appeasing body language, staying down but trying to lick the adult's mouth. These two are a good match in terms of communicating their feelings and will need minimal management.

LOW AROUSAL INTRODUCTIONS

Helping Out

Initially without contact:

- Ensure there is an exchange of personal smells (this could be an exchange of bedding).
- Allow them to see each other – but not make contact.
- Allow them to hear each other.
- When arousal and interest is low, proceed to...

A more stimulating environment

- Make sure encounters are kept brief.
- Be in a position to separate, keeping everything as calm as possible.
- When arousal and interest in each other is low, proceed to...

More contact:

- Be prepared to help out if one of the pair gets over-excited or seems worried.

Curiosity drives this puppy – with head and ears up, he wants to approach.

tolerate or, more probably, to enjoy each other. So for that particular relationship, little long-term damage is done.

However, this is your puppy's first experience of meeting a 'new' dog and if those first encounters were fraught, it will be indelibly imprinted on his brain. He will carry that emotion to subsequent encounters with new dogs, so the impact could be long-lived.

On his next meeting, we neither want him feeling that he will be able to jump all over the new dog, nor that it might be a frightening or threatening encounter. It, therefore, pays enormous dividends if we take care and allow time to ensure that his very first introduction to a 'new' dog goes well.

As the pushchair nears, he takes a step back. But he stretches his head forward showing he is still keen to investigate.

SEEING THROUGH YOUR DOG'S EYES

With a puppy, or a dog that has limited social experience, you need to be sensitive to the way he views the world. You need to be aware of what has gone before and gradually build up his bank of experience so that nothing fazes him. Dogs with limited experience, because of youth or lack of exposure, can find people who don't look 'normal' disquieting.

Looking through your dog's eyes, a person wearing a helmet or carrying a rucksack does not fit the normal human shape. Equally, someone sitting on a bench or

As the pushchair goes past, he approaches more closely and appears more confident. However, his ears are back and he is stretching forward, telling us of his on-going uncertainty. (See this puppy again in Chapter 9).

LIFE IS A JOURNEY – NOT A DESTINATION

You may feel that a puppy is desperately in need of socialisation to overcome his hesitant start, but this will only be productive if it is done sympathetically. Take a look at the table (below) to work out how much novelty a puppy can tolerate, and how to progress his education.

BEHAVIOUR IN A NEW SITUATION	GREEN LIGHT	AMBER LIGHT	RED LIGHT
EXPLORING	Keenly and freely into everything.	Keen but often hesitant, lots of approaching and retreating.	Reluctant, backing off.
RECOVERY FROM BEING STARTLED	Immediate.	A few seconds.	5 plus seconds.
SO...	Go for it. But make sure you are the most interesting thing around!	Protect him from being overwhelmed. Build confidence by slowing down experiences/novelty. Keep repeating experiences.	Make sure most of what you explore is familiar to him and has pleasant associations. Go on lots of mini walks, with just a little novelty.

lying on the grass looks very different to the 'normal' walking people he sees, especially if has picked up a scent or heard sounds before seeing a visual image. As for a torso, with a head and arms but no body, seen in a workman half below the pavement, or on the other side of a wall...

To us humans it is obvious that these are people, but a dog sees like a dog and will need similar or related experiences to make sense of these unusual sights. A well-adjusted puppy will react to new experiences but will have a quick recovery time, suffering only a fleeting loss of confidence. However, the overwhelmed puppy and the less confident puppy need to be socialised in a highly structured manner, proceeding with care and caution.

If your puppy's exploratory behaviour and his recovery rate are giving you the green light (see table above), walking down a busy street may be an appropriate experience.

If your puppy is responding with amber behaviours, you will help him to habituate more easily if you walk on quiet streets for shorter periods, and return to that street several times. Providing there is only a few seconds of apprehension, his concern will soon be forgotten as he bounces back to his normal behaviour.

The puppy that is showing red light behaviours will become more worried and stressed if too much is asked of him, so you need to delay his exposure to a busy street situation until he has grown in confidence in many easier settings.

Dogs make strong associations if they have been fearful or in pain. Take the youngster who injured his hind leg, and had to be examined by a number of vets and specialists to diagnose the problem. All these examinations were conducted when the dog was in pain. As a result, when the dog was grown up, he was relaxed and happy with his family, but he was seriously aggressive with strangers.

It is also important to be aware of your own reactions. If your puppy was attacked by a dog that looked like a large, black Labrador, you would probably become tense and be worried every time your dog is approached by a dog of a similar type. This, in itself, will have a bearing on how your dog reacts; unintentionally you can prime him to expect a problem, and this is bound to affect the way he behaves.

During this formative period of development, it is crucial to protect a youngster from being overwhelmed, but knowing when to draw the line will be different for each dog. Too much intervention from an owner can be just as damaging. For example, a small dog who is continually picked up by his owner is denied a full range of experiences. As a result, the dog is slow to learn the social skills to cope and communicate. However, if a puppy – regardless of size – is overwhelmed by a situation, and is showing no signs of recovery within a period of 5-10 seconds, your job is to extract him from that situation as soon as possible. He will need at least 24 hours in his home environment to give him the opportunity to fully recover before taking him out again.

As the puppy moves from mild concern to acceptance, he will soon perceive that this situation holds no threats for him. By experiencing lots of low

Transfixed by the sight before him, this Leonberger puppy sits down while he tries to make sense of it. A loose tail and upright ears, combined with panting, tells us he isn't frightened. His owner reads the situation correctly, and gives him the time he needs.

level stresses that he quickly recovers from, the better his bounce-back and resilience will be throughout his life. The more often he experiences the period of recovery or 'bounce back', the more confident he will become. He will then be able to generalise his reaction and apply it to any new situation he comes across. While a nervous puppy's progress will be ultimately limited by his genetic wiring, experiences that are carefully tailored to his emotional make up can make dramatic inroads to maximizing his potential.

A puppy that has poor coping skills initially may, with the right structure and support, overcome his early difficulties entirely. Although there is no doubt that, for some dogs, a degree of fear and nervousness is in their genetic make up, which means they will be more likely to resort to this type of behaviour when under pressure. However, gentle socialisation at the puppy's pace – however slow that may need to be – and ensuring positive outcomes, will go a long way towards minimising this tendency.

What happens if your puppy is exposed to a negative experience, despite all your best efforts? What if, out of the blue, a strange dog runs up to your puppy and bowls him over. How traumatic is this experience?

To an extent, this is governed by the puppy's genetically engineered recovery rate, which gives him the ability to 'shake off' a bad experience without leaving a lasting impression. It is also significantly influenced by his previous experiences. If he has had lots of pleasant encounters, a one-off negative encounter will be less salient and have less impact. If, for example, he has already met 20 dogs without stress or difficulty, he will have built up some resilience and will be better able to withstand the negative experience. In the same way, if the first person a puppy meets is loud-mouthed and rough, he may worry that all people he meets are likely to behave like this.

In the run up to adolescence, and throughout the 'teenage' period, hormone levels will change and a youngster may, again, show signs of being worried and apprehensive – even when confronting something that he has formerly accepted without a qualm. Reactions vary from individual to individual, but, typically, the older pup will come across something that previously seemed innocuous – a statue in the street or a rubbish bin – and decide it is scary. He will raise his hackles, lower his body posture and may inch towards it. Alternatively, he may try a more up-front challenge and bark at the offending object – repeatedly advancing and then retreating as fear takes over.

Being aware of this developmental phase can give you confidence to slow down, or even have a break from socialising for several months, or until your puppy is enjoying and seeking out novelty again. Soldiering on is rarely as successful.

LOOK AND LISTEN

A strong, fearful reaction is easy to pick up on, but what about the more subtle signs that tell you how your dog is feeling? When you are out and about, your aim is to get to a destination. Your focus is elsewhere, and it is easy to miss some of the all-important clues. For example, what is your puppy's body language telling you when you walk him on the lead? How relaxed and natural is he?

- Is he taking in the environment, sniffing, exploring and perhaps casually looking around, then keeping pace with you as you move off?
- Is he hanging back, unsure of the situation, and trying to avoid being pulled towards it?
- Is he robotically marching along on a lovely, loose lead but too afraid to sniff and investigate, afraid to tell you what he would like to do? If this is the case, he will hold his head upright, or low and forward, his body, his tail and his ears will be tense, and his lips will be tight.
- Is he almost hugging the walls with his body and tail lowered?
- Is he pulling? Is this to get to the park and meet other dogs, or to be off lead as soon as possible? Perhaps your lead-walk training is causing him concern? Or is it all too much for him, and he's pulling to get home where he feels safe?
- When is he hesitant? When does he elect to sit and watch?
- Does he skirt around particular obstacles? Would he rather not walk on the roadside?
- Where and why might he hang back?
- Where and why he might not do his normal exploring behaviours?
- If he pulls, is it when he's trying to pass something that worries him?

TIME WELL SPENT

If a puppy is continually put into a situation where he feels backing off/avoiding behaviours don't work, he will, increasingly use more defensive and proactive strategies.

You therefore need to find a way to introduce him to new situations much more slowly, finding a way to dilute them so he never feels a loss of confidence.

Five one-minute experiences (with breaks in-between), which are pleasant and non-challenging, will be far more productive in building confidence both in the short-term and, just as importantly, in the long-term, than exposing a worried puppy to a situation for half an hour in which the important first five minutes were daunting.

Early interactions are so important: Trying to get away from the adult dog, this pup has a negative experience with his new owner, as well as his new canine companion.

Watch him listen to him, and take notice. Can you make the walk more enjoyable for both of you? Could you walk on the other side of the road, or not go past that particular house. Or maybe not even do that particular walk for now? There is a lot he is telling you – it is up to you to listen.

SUMMING UP

Your puppy is an individual; how you respond to him and what experiences you expose him to should be tailored to him alone. The more you can read his body language and are aware of what he finds difficult and stressful, the more you can structure his experiences so he is always growing in confidence and is, increasingly, developing into your dream dog.

Chapter Three

TO LOVE AND TO BE LOVED

Is it reciprocated?

A dictionary definition of love is: "to have great attachment to, and affection for." The relationship most owners have with their dogs easily fulfills these criteria, and although dogs do not share our emotional range, there is no doubting their devotion to us – or our devotion to them. The difference is in the way we express our love and, here, we can fall into a minefield of miscommunication.

FORMS OF ATTACHMENT

There are some dogs – and some breeds in particular – that form a particular bond with one member of the family, and their need is focused on being with that one, special person. German Shepherds are well known for forming strong attachments, and many of the small, Toy breeds, such as Poodles and Papillons, may focus their attention on one person. When this key person is absent, there will be a noticeable change in behaviour; the dog will often be more subdued, or he may become unusually clingy with someone else.

Attachment to individual family members can vary depending on what is going on, what the dog's needs are at a particular time, and what that person is bringing to the relationship. There may be one person who is the provider, and is responsible for food and walks, so the dog will be more tuned into them when these opportunities present themselves.

There may be a contact person; the one who gives attention by petting and stroking. Some dogs find this contact very important and will rely on this person both physically and emotionally. There are the touchy/feely breeds like the little Cavalier King Charles Spaniel, and many of the larger short-coated breeds, such as Weimaraners, Dalmatians, and Pointers, who gain security from physical contact. In contrast some dogs – particularly breeds such as Border Collies and Working Sheepdogs, Bearded Collies and Briards – may not particularly like or need a lot of physical contact, but they very much want to be involved in all that is going on within the family.

A dog may form another, different attachment with a family member who tends to be slightly rough and heavy-handed in their approach. The dog may become very needy around this person, often showing appeasing, submissive behaviour, which is often mistakenly interpreted as the dog loving this person more than anyone else. He will by highly excited when he greets his 'special' person, perhaps being excessively wriggly or there may be highly energised mouthing or jumping up. The dog's desire to lick, especially towards the face, will be more apparent than with other family members he feels more comfortable with. There is no doubting the attachment; the dog has formed a strong bond, but he is still worried. This is seen by his body posture which will be lowered, with dipped neck and shoulders, and he will frequently turn his head to one side - away from the person that worries him. See Rough-housing: Does your dog really want it? (page 47)

UNREQUITED LOVE

As you read your dog's body language and understand what he is feeling, it will become increasingly apparent that the 'when', 'where' and 'by whom' is extremely important. The dog that leans ecstatically into you for an ear rub, or stretches his neck up for you to scratch, or presents his back or his loins for a massage will not do this in all situations. What he considered to be bliss at home may be unwanted when he is in a novel situation, or when there is interesting stimulus that distracts him. If your dog has other things on his mind, be it wanting to sniff, play, run, investigate, or if he's a bit worried about another person or another dog, your petting and fussing may be too much, even to the point where he finds it punishing.

SEE WHAT HE SAYS

What is your dog's favourite way of being touched by you? Now try fussing him in this way in different situations and fine-tune your ability to observe his facial expressions and body language.

Try petting him:

- At home when all is calm.
- Just after the window cleaner or postman have called.
- When you are about to let him off-lead.
- Out on a walk in a boring place (stand or sit still for a couple of minutes first).
- On a walk when you know his focus will be elsewhere.
- In the middle of a training or play session when he is focused on a toy.

Watch carefully and monitor the times and situations where he loves physical contact, the times when he tolerates it, and the times when he ducks away from your touch or moves away from you.

LOVING YOUR DOG

In the name of affection you kiss, hug, squeeze and pat your dog, showing just as much demonstrative feeling as you would to another person. But what does this mean to your dog? You are showing your love for him, but does he feel loved by these displays of affection? Possibly not.

KISSING

We tend to liken licking to kissing because if you kiss a dog on the face he will lick you back – preferably aiming for your mouth or nose – and you feel your kiss is being returned. When two dogs meet, they may momentarily lick each other, but this is relatively uncommon. It is more likely to occur if one dog feels uncertain and attempts to lick around the other dog's mouth. This is exactly what happens when a person is involved. Your approach – bringing your face to your dog's – leads to an appeasement display, i.e. trying to lick your mouth. Look at the rest of your dog's face and body. Is it soft and happy as you would expect if you kissed a child? Or is it a bit tight and submissive? Is it relaxed, slow and gentle or quick and intense? Does he show any avoidance, or does he show relief in the form of a body shake or a lick of his lips when you move away?

KISS OR CRINGE

You may be kissing your dog because you love him, but most dogs will respond by trying to turn away or back off. Intense or fast licking is an attempt to placate or appease – don't fool yourself that it is the equivalent of an affectionate human kiss...

As this German Shepherd pulls away, he shortens his neck and does a tongue lick.

Note the tightness of the Cavalier's jaw and mouth; the tongue out suggests an appeasing lick. The wide eyes may be more indicative of the breed than concern, or maybe not...

36

Here is our Jack Russell who has the confused relationship with her male owner (see pages 8 and 19). She feels threatened so gives the early stages of a snarly warning while, at the same time, licking her owner's mouth in an attempt to placate him.

As the owner gets a little more serious and takes her paw, she feels even more threatened. She continues to try and lick to appease him, she moves her body back to avoid him, and she shows more of her teeth in an attempt to make him back off. What a dilemma she is in.

HUGGING

What is the nearest thing to a hug in dog-to-dog communication? Perhaps the bitch using her chin to nudge her week-old puppies close to her for cleaning? You may see it in big-dog/little-dog play with one dog pressing into the other but other than that, it doesn't happen. In fact hugging most closely resembles a pre-fight challenge when a dog uses his front body weight to pin the other dog's head over his shoulders. You may also see a clasp and squeeze when one dog mounts another. Some dogs will tolerate this by standing still, others will try to move away, and there are some who will quickly flip around trying to warn the other dog. When confronted by a hugging human, a dog will use the same strategies in a bid to gain some personal space. While some dogs may tolerate a hug, very few enjoy it – watch your dog's body language before and after...

PATTING/STROKING/RUBBING

With the exception of patting, these ways of showing love and affection are easier for your dog to make sense of. Dogs that are good friends and are very relaxed with each other may clean one another – especially the ears (this is also where most dogs enjoy a rub). Many dogs will lick and clean themselves or each other as part of their settling down routine. This is very different to the appeasing lick – it is slow, long and deep.

When you are stroking your dog, be careful how and where you stroke. Watch to see which areas he likes best or if there are ways you stroke that he doesn't enjoy – perhaps you are stroking too vigorously, perhaps for too long, or rubbing the coat in the wrong direction. If it is too arousing his movements will speed up; if he is worried he may use avoidance techniques such as turning his head or his body away, licking, yawning, blinking and maybe even shaking you off. Now try patting him on his head. Almost certainly he will let you know he doesn't like that; that is, if you care to listen with your eyes. He will duck a bit; probably blink and his ears will be tense.

HORRIBLE HUGS

These five dogs are giving different clues which show they are not happy about being hugged.

A tongue flick and wide eyes of the dog (pictured left) paints a clear picture. The dog (pictured right) is holding his ears back and low. He is holding his body away from his owner and looking into the distance.

A two-faced look with the head leaning away. The eyes and ears are disjointed: the eye and ear of one side is directed to where he wants to be.

Small dogs generally get the roughest deal when it comes to the human version of showing love. A small or Toy dog is frequently picked up (making it much harder to observe whole-body communication), kissed, hugged, squeezed, and encouraged through mouth kissing to show lots of appeasing licking gestures. Most little dogs love being close to their owners so they learn to tolerate the unpleasant bits in order to maintain the physical contact.

It is not unusual for a little dog to relax and sleep in his owner's lap but, on the other hand, to develop such intolerance to kissing, hugging and squeezing that he ends up biting their face. If only that owner had read their dog's body language from the outset; historically he would have tried turning his face away or gone stiff. When his signals went unheeded, he was forced to escalate his behaviour to growling then biting. Your dog may want to sit beside you, or on you, but that does not necessarily mean he wants you to fuss him.

The tightly held back lips and wide eyes exaggerate this Bullmastiff's wrinkles. His ears are back and he is leaning away.

The lowered neck and very tightly held mouth of this dog belie his apparent tolerance. It looks as if he has shut down/given up.

SHOWING AFFECTION

It is not wrong to demonstrate the love you feel for your dog, but it must be in a way he understands and feels comfortable with. Observe your dog's body language to find out what it is he likes, what he tolerates or what he dislikes. Bear in mind: 'enjoy' is not the same as 'tolerate'– and although there are some very tolerant breeds and individuals – you should never make assumptions.

BUT MY DOG ASKS FOR AFFECTION...

There are some dogs who want physical contact with their owner, either by being touched, being beside them, or being on their lap. This can be highly pleasurable for both dog and owner. However, there are probably many more dogs who seek physical contact but, at some point, become worried or even frightened. Your well-intended demonstrations of affection are perceived as being confusing or threatening.

To reduce this perceived threat, the dog will show increasingly submissive or appeasing behaviours which we humans so frequently misconstrue. You might think your dog is asking for your affection but, in reality, he might be doing everything he can to placate you. If you monitor his reactions closely, you will be able to spot the difference. These behaviours are the outward manifestation of your dog's emotional state of mind at that particular time.

If, through his behaviour, he is pleading the equivalent of: "I'm only a puppy - please, please be nice to me" or "I'm sorry, I'm sorry, I'm sorry", you risk doing two things. Firstly, by responding to his plea you ingrain the behaviour. It gets repeated again and again, and intensifies, as he seeks and gets reassurance. But perhaps more importantly, this type of interaction substantiates his emotional unworthiness. It is as though you are saying: "Yes, you are the lowest of the low; yes, I want you to humble yourself at my feet; yes, I am in charge here – creep and crawl in my presence". Every time you respond, the self-confidence and emotional robustness of your dog is challenged. He is not being given the scope to become more relaxed and self-assured; you are effectively stunting his personality. However, it doesn't need to be this way.

GIVING LOVE...

These youngsters are naturally affectionate to their dogs – but the dogs are making it clear that they are not enjoying it.

Can you see the disjointed orientation of this Golden Retriever's eyes and of his ears? Where is his nose pointing?

This Border Terrier looks quite relaxed but what is he avoiding with his front paws and why does he feel the need to behave like this? We need to know more to make a judgement.

Which way is this Shepherd leaning? What are his ears doing?

A very compromised dog. This was almost certainly a fast and sudden head turn towards the child by way of a warning. What is his tail saying? What a good dog to have stopped himself from biting – I wonder if he was listened to?

CHOOSE SENSITIVELY

Choose when to respond and show affection. Choose how to respond and show affection:

WHEN

You need to try to avoid putting your dog in situations where he shows concern. If you observe closely, you will see which situations trigger this type of behaviour – behaviour you probably won't see at any other time. You do not want to endorse or encourage his feeling of neediness. The best strategy is not to respond when he is showing appeasing behaviour but be quick to interact when he appears more composed and self-assured.

HOW

Do what your dog likes you to do – touches and interactions that lead to confident, relaxed behaviours.

If he's showing needy, appeasing behaviours:

- Your body language should suggest that you haven't noticed his neediness; there should be no sense that you are rejecting him or that you are annoyed with him.
- Slowly turn away from him or take a step or two backwards or sideways, thus helping him to get out of the sit or from being on his back.
- Approach and touch without going over the top of

him with your hand or body.

- Keep your stroking slow and calm, not vigorous and stimulating.
- If he still shows concern, avoid touching him until his confidence in you gradually develops.

If you are holding a little, needy dog, you should probably turn your face well away. Do not ask for, or encourage, those appeasing licks at your mouth. Making eye contact, talking or touching may help or may exaggerate his behaviours further. A dog that is mildly or moderately worried or frightened needs you to maintain your relaxed, casual body language but not respond to his needy behaviours. You may need to moderate when and how you respond in order to increase his enjoyment and build his confidence.

Evidence of relaxation and confidence	Evidence of stress/fear
Slow, minimal movement	Faster, excessive movement
No muscle tension	Tension in limbs and neck
Tail/back/rear relaxed, with a gentle tail wag	The top or the entire tail may be tucked/rear wriggling with low tail wag
Stands or sits casually If he rolls over, neck, head and legs are floppy and relaxed	May do a non-taught tail-tucked sit, roll over on his back with tense neck and legs, may urinate
Flopped against you	Pushed hard against, or on you
Soft eyes and ears	Tight ears, blinking wide eyes
Relaxed mouth	Closed tight mouth or licking
No aim	Aiming for your face, particularly your mouth
Starts and ends seamlessly	Starts and ends with increased energy

REWARDING OR PUNISHING?

Your class trainer may be encouraging you to praise and physically interact with your dog as a means of rewarding him. But it is only by observing his response that you can tell whether he finds it rewarding.

If he is only tolerating your attention (or worse still, ducking or moving from it) you are not only failing to praise him in a way he understands, but he is unlikely to repeat the behaviour you have been trying to teach. He will only repeat the desired behaviour if he feels truly rewarded.

YOUR EMOTIONAL NEED

Dogs, especially needy dogs, can bring out the nurturing element in all of us. Puppies, in particular, trigger biochemical changes that will influence your response. The maternal hormones may literally flow, but you need to be careful not to be a 'smother lover', not to think you are loving, while actually you are unintentionally diminishing your dog's confidence by encouraging and reinforcing needy, appeasing behaviours, or ignoring what he likes and dislikes. Ask yourself:

- Is it really love if it the recipient doesn't want it?
- Is it really love if it makes the recipient apologetic and appeasing?
- Is it really love if the recipient's feelings are ignored?

You need to be brave enough to acknowledge why you pet and fuss your dog – and find out from him how you can do it better.

We owe it to future generations to help them see and understand this tongue flick.

MAKING CONTACT EASIER FOR YOUR DOG

In these photos, the dogs look more comfortable than those in the previous pages, even if somewhat appeasing. What are the owners doing, or not doing, that releases the dog?

While the Jack Russell is being held and stared at, she tries to turn her head away and does a lip lick. Note the tongue is also directed away.

Bending over a dog can be intimidating. The owner has avoided this by simply crouching down to welcome his puppy.

It is when the owner's head is turned (perhaps to look at the photographer or perhaps in response to a lick) that the Jack Russell stretches upwards and licks appeasingly. But look at her eyes, ears, mouth and whiskers. They are much softer and less tense.

This little Dachshund is being held in a sensitive manner so he can look outwards and does not have to endure eye-to-eye contact. His 'leaning in' body language tells us how comfortable he is with his owner. The slight tension in his eyes and mouth are probably due to the presence of the photographer.

GREETINGS IN THE FAMILY

When owners were asked what they liked most about their dogs, the almost unanimous response was the way their dogs greeted them. You know that when you come through the door, even if you have had the worst of days, and you are in the foulest of tempers, your dog will still think you are wonderful and will be delighted to see you. This is one of the great pleasures of owning a dog, and it answers a very real need in all of us. However you can go one step further and, by observing how a dog greets you and other members of the family, you can find out what he is really thinking and feeling.

DURATION OF GREETINGS

The duration of greeting behaviour can vary widely between individuals. With some dogs, the hellos are said and, after a minute or so, they go and settle without seeking further attention. Others dogs are much more persistent. There are several reasons for this. Firstly, it is dependent on a dog's energy; a high-energy dog is always going to prolong any form of activity. It is also to do with a dog's experience. It may be that he has been greeted by someone in the family who has gone overboard – playing with him and fussing him – so he has learnt to continue his greeting behaviour to elicit this type of response.

The duration of a greeting will also be influenced by how a dog feels when he is left. If he is anxious when family members are absent, or if he is particularly attached to one member of the family, there will be a build up of tension and his greeting behaviour will be prolonged and exaggerated when he is reunited.

A dog who struggles to cope on his own will experience great relief when the family members return, and this can be expressed in different ways. He may show submissive, appeasing behaviour which tends to be more energised, more prolonged, and harder to redirect. A less stressed dog may be relieved by jumping up and stretching against you, possibly yawning at the same time.

There will be other, small indicators of the anxiety he has experienced in your absence. He may go and get the chew you gave him when you left, which remained uneaten until his anxiety lifted on your return. He may go and have a long drink from his water bowl, as he has been panting but has been too stressed to drink in your absence. He may have had access to the garden, but he will only go out and toilet when you return.

No matter how important these things are to him, the ritual of greeting must take priority. If your dog has been anxious in your absence, he may be very clingy when you come back. He will follow you from room to room, intent on not letting you out of his sight.

You may find your dog only gives a brief greeting and then goes to lie down on his own as if you are being punished for leaving him, but a dog is not capable of this level of reasoning. In this situation, he is simply expressing a huge sense of relief. He has been so stressed while you have been away that he has mentally exhausted himself. It is only when you return that he can afford to relax and settle for a much-needed sleep.

SMELLS RIGHT

For dogs, scent plays a vital part in recognition and has far greater significance than visual appearance. This can be seen clearly if a scent has changed or is disguised in some way. For example, if a key person has been absent for some time, and has undergone a change, such as being treated for a medical problem or is hormonally different, e.g. pregnant, the dog may be momentarily confused by the change in the odour they are giving off.

IGNORING YOUR DOG

This can be a useful strategy to reduce greeting time arousal in excitable and/or appeasing dogs, providing:

- Your dog doesn't feel he is being rejected. Be casual in your approach and reward him with calm attention.
- You help him to learn, and enjoy, a more appropriate greeting behaviour.

Loving your dog is about listening to him, finding out what he likes and dislikes, and responding in ways that nurture his confidence and calmness.

The dog will greet the person, and even though the voice and body language are familiar, the all-important scent does not ring true. The dog has to process this – which may take a few seconds, or even a few minutes – before recognition dawns. On an everyday level, your dog may give you a second sniff – or he may snort – if you come back from the hairdresser smelling of hair spray, or if you have tried on a new perfume. You smell familiar but there is a different, unfamiliar smell that he needs to process.

GREETING KEY PEOPLE

Dogs that live in a family will give a special greeting to all members – but does the person who feeds or trains the dog get a different reaction? Without doubt, a key person will get a different greeting, but we also need to look at the habits this person has created on returning.

For example, if someone comes in and greets the dog quietly and calmly, the dog is likely to respond in a similar manner. This does not mean the dog has a lesser relationship with this individual – it may be the key person in his life – but he is simply reflecting and responding to the greeting that he gets from this person.

As we have seen, the more exaggerated greetings are often directed towards someone the dog does not feel so comfortable with.

NOISE BASED GREETINGS

A lot of dogs are excited when they greet their family, but use minimal contact and rely more on vocalisation which may take the form of whistling, whining, squeaking, howling and barking. There are dogs who use exaggerated movement, such as repeatedly bouncing on their front paws and then moving away, often accompanied by barking. They may also circle the person they are greeting, signaling a degree of uncertainty. Barking expresses excitement but some breeds, and some individuals, are more prone than others. It is interesting to consider how much your own vocalisation will affect a dog's response. If you verbally 'gee up' the dog, he will become increasingly vocal as his excitement escalates. This may make you feel good, but it does little to induce feelings of calmness in the dog and can become the trigger for increasingly over the top behaviour.

GIFT BEARERS

The gundog breeds, most particularly Labradors and Golden Retrievers, and some Cocker Spaniels, have a desperate need to have something – anything – in their mouths when they are greeting their loved ones. You will even see a dog heading in the wrong direction – away from their family – to pick up a toy, a sock, or a shoe, so they have something to parade with. There are many dogs – other than gundogs – who also seem to be happier if they have something in their mouth when arousal levels increase. It gives their excitement a positive outlet rather than having to direct it towards people. In this situation, the dog does not want to give the item to you; in fact, taking a 'gift' can result in a confused and worried response. Watch out for the dog backing away, turning his head away, wide eyes and a low, fast moving tail. He will be much more comfortable if you confine your response to effusive admiration!

SMALL DOG SYNDROME

Toy dogs have been bred for centuries to be lapdogs, living in very close proximity with people, and they show a great deal of facial awareness. As a result the greetings they give will be very different than larger breeds. In many instances, it involves being picked up and so there is a lot of facial contact. Owners often encourage this, asking for a "kiss" which, as

we have seen, can lead to appeasement behaviour. Again, observation is key. Does your dog welcome it and enjoy the interaction or are there signs that he is worried, such as neck shortening, head held down or ears held tight? Although there are many small dogs who do not relish this close contact, there are certainly others who accept it, and may even seek it out. Whether they actually enjoy it, or if it is more a matter of learned helplessness, is for you to observe.

HIGH-ENERGY GREETINGS

Owners of Pointers, Boxers and Bearded Collies will probably be familiar with this one! This is the dog who bounces from the floor right up to your face in one easy movement. The aim is to get to your face – mouth nose and ears – as this is perceived as the most important part of you. The desire to do this may be increased by your own response, and the dog's reaction to it. This high energy greeting starts as a means of getting contact but it often develops into a bounce on, and then off you, as the dog is rejected or reprimanded. Sometimes the bounce becomes higher and more exaggerated, or without any contact at all – the dog simply bounces around you.

Another form of high-energy greeting is the dog that continually spins or circles around his owner. This is often seen in Border Collies, German Shepherds and Staffordshire Bull Terriers. A Collie will use his herding instinct to circle round and round you. Spinning will be at high speed, usually in front of you. This can sometimes develop into obsessive behaviour, particularly if an owner increases

A visible, tangible measure of how much energy this Terrier puts into his greeting – even before his owner is present.

anxiety by reprimanding greeting behaviours. In a worst-case scenario, the owner may, intentionally or unintentionally, encourage the dog to chase his tail. The obsessive nature of spinning triggers the release of endorphins, which makes the dog feel good. He is therefore more likely to repeat the behaviour and apply it to other situations he finds exciting, such as at mealtimes, waiting to go out of a door, or waiting to have the lead attached.

High-energy dogs feed off our responses. The more noise you make, the noisier your dog will be, if your movements are fast and manic, the dog will reflect this and will bounce and jump up, shedding all inhibitions. If you invite contact – grabbing the dog and pushing him away – he will increase his contact and will start mouthing. The danger of this high level of arousal is that it can easily go too far. Some dogs can cope with this degree of anarchy, but it may have serious implications for a nervous dog who will become increasingly worried by the unpredictability of the situation, or the person, and may generalise his suspicion to the whole human race!

Big greetings can also cause a problem in dogs that have issues with separation. The dog will be effusive when his owner returns, but if this is encouraged and expounded upon, it has the potential to increase his anxiety. He has lost everything when his owner goes, but when the owner returns, everything is wonderful – and so the highs and lows become hugely exaggerated, thus exacerbating the whole problem.

"PLEASE LOVE ME!"

The dog who is submissive and appeasing will keep a low body posture, ducking his neck and shoulders. Sometimes, the ducking may be minimal but there will be a lot of wriggling behaviour, commonly seen in the Spaniel breeds, and some of the Retrievers, although they may not be so exaggerated. This type of dog is actively seeking physical contact. A more extreme example is a dog who sits as though its rear end was glued to the floor. This has not been trained – although owners may reinforce it by giving the verbal cue – but is an emotionally induced sit and has different body language when compared with a trained sit. This is a high-energy sit, and it is as if the dog is making huge efforts to inhibit his behaviour. In some cases, it may be accompanied by submissive urination, showing a

Mixed messages: The Border Collie is choosing to make contact. However, the tightly drawn back lips, the ears held back and the avoidance of eye contact suggest a dog in conflict.

combination of both fear and excitement.

At its most exaggerated, the dog rolls over and may also submissively urinate. We are not very good at interpreting this behaviour as we tend to fuss these types of dogs. But the more you fuss them, the more the behaviour will continue and the more exaggerated it will become. The ears are pinned back; in fact, everything is pinned back and tense. Compare the soft, relaxed body language a dog shows when he is settled beside you – rolling over to have his chest and belly rubbed – with the tense limbs, tucked tail, and neck pushed into the floor of the worried dog who rolls over when greeting.

The greeting roll-over is not a: "please rub my tummy". It is much more submissive: "I'm only little, you can rub my tummy if you need to". Tracing back to wolf ancestry, the dog is showing he poses no threat, but we humans tend to crash through the true meaning of this behaviour. Our instinctive reaction is to rub the dog's tummy when, in fact, he needs space. We should be reinforcing his confident behaviours not acknowledging his insecurity.

44

FROM APPEASING TO TRUSTING

No self-respecting owner wants a dog who continually feels the need to appease. The aim is to establish a relationship that is based on trust. There are ways you can facilitate this when your are interacting with him:

- Avoid making any movements towards the appeasing dog when he comes to greet you.
- Calmly back away and turn aside.

Can he maintain confident postures and behaviours if you:

- Look at him?
- Gently talk to him?
- Nod towards him?
- Advance your hands towards him (initially, try under his chin and ears).

You have hit the right level if, when you move away, he calmly comes to you asking for more, quietly settles, or even moves off. If he does a sudden, fast movement, adjust how you are interacting with him.

CONFUSING THE PICTURE

As we have seen, dogs have a great need to greet and re-establish affiliations. However, we humans can confuse the picture so the dog becomes unsure of himself. This can happen very easily; your dog is barking or whining, jumps up at you, or has picked up your best shoe, and you immediately reprimand him. He has gone into the situation with the most positive of intentions. His chief desire is to greet you and be accepted – and then his overtures are rejected. In most cases, this exaggerates the dog's behaviour; the more he feels rejected the more he will try to elicit a reassuring response. If he is greeting someone who does not want to be licked or sniffed, he may well sense this and will redouble his efforts.

The same thing happens if you ignore a greeting dog because he is barking or whining in the belief that it will stop the behaviour. In reality, an insecure dog feels increasingly worried by your non-reaction; his behaviour intensifies and he becomes increasingly needy. The consequences of rejecting greetings is something we should be deeply aware of, particularly with young dogs who are learning behaviours and developing attitudes that will last a lifetime.

SUMMING UP

There are lots of different ways to demonstrate your love for your dog, but not all of these will be loved by your dog. Bear in mind the following:

- Despite our desire to do so, kissing, hugging and petting isn't naturally understood by dogs.
- Small avoidance behaviours, such as turning/looking away and lip licking, indicate a discomfort, as does an appeasing roll over or a high-energy outburst following interaction.
- Different greeting behaviours reflect different relationships.
- Highly excitable or tense, appeasing behaviours suggest much less trust and confidence than more relaxed greetings.

By being aware, and adjusting your interactions according to how the dog responds – before, during and after – he can love being loved by you.

If we only stood back, we could see what our dogs have to say.

Chapter Four

IT'S PLAYTIME!

Understanding the game

Play is a vital component of learning for virtually all young mammals as it gives them a chance to learn the skills that are needed in adult life. But when an animal reaches maturity, the need to play is substituted by the real thing – the need to survive. A puppy under six months has a massive need to play; it literally preoccupies every waking minute. As he grows up he will, increasingly, be content to be part of what is going on rather than having an incessant desire to play. But unlike his wolf ancestors, the domesticated dog does not have to focus on survival – and most no longer have to work for a living. So where does this leave play?

The decision to play is a free choice – you and your dog are engaging in play because you want to, not because you have to. This is time you choose to be with each other, interacting and communicating, one-to-one. It is a bonding experience for both you and your dog but, as with all interactions, it is a two-way street. You have to find a way of playing that your dog is completely comfortable with; he has to learn to adapt his play so that it is appropriate for you – his human playmate.

GAMES WITH TOYS

The type of play dogs engage in is often directly related to their breed and genetic make up. There are some breeds and breed types that gain an almost ecstatic pleasure from being able to play using their breed trait. The hound types love to run but are not that fussed about owning or bringing back a ball. A Spaniel will be intent on hunting for a toy whereas a Collie, with his strong herding instinct, is focused on the chase. The retrieving breeds are obsessed with carrying and retrieving.

These traits spill over into other forms of behaviour as well as play. The tougher, guarding type breeds will be single-minded and appear quite thick-skinned if anyone tries to divert them from their game. Most breeds enjoy playing tug with a toy, but for the terriers and bull breeds, the joy is in tugging and holding on, which goes back to their hunting and fighting ancestry. Shaking and tearing often accompanies this form of play. Playing tug games used to be frowned upon in the past as it was thought to encourage more aggressive instincts. But we now understand that play, as long as it is controlled, fulfils a real need in the dog and can also be a useful tool in training.

A dog needs to be able to control his level of arousal: to come up, and to come down. Playing with a toy is a useful way to learn this, as well as giving you practice in moderating his arousal. The dog has the excitement of the game, but we can teach him to adjust his arousal by doing something calm, such as being asked to sit periodically throughout the game,

Even though it's a bone rather than a toy that's involved, we can see by the Jack Russell's open back legs, forward ears and covered teeth that these two are playing.

46

or to find some scattered treats when the game comes to an end. The dog practices controlling his arousal levels and this is invaluable in many situations, most particularly in a family with small children where a dog cannot be allowed to run riot.

Play can also be a very useful way of redirecting behaviour, giving the dog a different focus. If a dog is mouthing or grabbing at his owner when he is excited, it can be the precursor to more aggressive behaviour. However, if the dog can be pre-emptively directed on to a toy, it can be used to manipulate arousal levels downwards. It can become a strategy for coping with potentially stressful situations, and, in time, to stop them developing in the first place.

NON-INTERACTIVE TOY USE

Parading around with a toy or item in the mouth can act as a stress-reliever or fidget-focus at times of high arousal. This is not an invitation to play, and play efforts on your part will not be appreciated. However, it is far better to encourage the mouthing of a toy than your hands, gloves, or best shoes.

Often a dog queuing for his run in agility, or any other dog sport, appreciates a toy in his mouth. He is aroused, but he cannot join in, so there is no obvious outlet for his heightened energy. It is therefore redirected to the toy. Whether this is an expression of excitement, frustration or, more worrying, an expression of stress, will depend on the individual dog. For some dogs, it is far better to focus on a toy rather than becoming even more stimulated – and frustrated. However, everything should be done to limit the dog's exposure to this degree of stress in the first place.

Many an adult pet dog seems perfectly happy without ever playing with his human family. But if your dog is stealing items to be chased by you, using other attention seeking behaviours, or chasing vehicles, birds or children, it needs redirecting. Channelling his mental and physical energy with more appropriate play can be part of the solution for many issues.

If a dog is possessive with toys or has behavioural issues relating to high levels of arousal, such as biting or grabbing his human playmate, play should be carefully structured to moderate arousal and make the correct, positive associations. Expert help may be necessary. Dogs who are having difficulties with arousal levels in other areas of their life should also be played with in a way that channels and allows practice of arousal control – not in a way that increases their arousal, or with the aim of simply tiring the dog.

This Sheltie redirects his high arousal/stress on to his toy. His teeth may be chattering.

Being a clown and fooling around with a toy might be a strategy to maintain relaxation and relieve stress, or maybe it's just something to do!

This tug is about gaining possession – the pull and all the dog's weight is directed downwards. Neither party is playing!

ENDING PLAY SESSIONS

For the play obsessed dog, play sessions must have a clear beginning and a clear end. We initiate the game, and we must end it, and this must be crystal clear to the dog otherwise we end up nurturing unwanted, attention-seeking behaviour. For the dog that continues to demand more play, the easiest solution is to walk away from the game. This may involve leaving your dog with the toy, but you are withdrawing the greater reward of playing with him. The value of the toy should depend on you playing with it and animating it, so withdrawing from the game will mean the toy is of no further interest. This will not be the case if you choose a toy that has intrinsic value for your dog – perhaps a rope that can be shredded or a squeaky toy – which provides its own reward, so it is best to avoid these kind of toys for interactive play.

A tongue flick, tight mouth, and with ears and eyes not focused on his owner, this Staffie is telling us that he is only tolerating the rough play.

ROUGH-HOUSING: DOES YOUR DOG REALLY WANT IT?

This type of contact play is not the exclusive preserve of the male members of a household, but there is no denying that it is more likely to be instigated by the more macho of owners. Rough play with puppies should always be avoided. It encourages biting and mouthing and, until we have an idea of the adult temperament, it is impossible to know what underlying issues we might be fuelling. Some dogs positively enjoy rough play; we can see from their body language that they are coping with complete confidence and are comfortable with the situation. The dog may be shoved back and forth, he may be encouraged to jump up and be pushed down, he may even be spun round in circles. However, for many dogs this introduces a fear element. The worried dog will show subtle signs of avoidance even while he is apparently joining in the game.

He will dive in only to retreat; he appears to interact but keeps turning away, his eyes briefly glancing in other directions. He has an air of tense anticipation because he is never sure what is coming next. It is clear that this dog is not enjoying the play sessions as much as his owner would like to think. This is particularly the case if the dog is lying on his back with his tail tightly tucked, and his ears set back. He is not asking for more play – even though he has not physically struggled or run away. Watch your dog carefully; he may well be signaling that he is not comfortable with what is going on.

For a dog, it is much harder to come to terms with fast, rough play. The human uses his hands to powerfully push and shove the dog's body or head away. The dog is flailing with just his mouth while having two human mouths (well, hands) to deal with. The movements are either fast or become faster. When two dogs are playing this increase in speed is often an indication of one dog feeling worried by being bullied by the other and frequently leads to the play ending in a fight. If the dog is rolled over, his tail will frequently be tightly tucked and he will fling himself into an upright position in preparation for further challenges. Exactly the same can be seen in rough play with humans – nearly always the dog will be using fearful, defensive body language.

The dog may come charging back for more; he will certainly be experiencing an adrenaline rush and he may well be addicted to this source for his adrenaline fix. Undoubtedly he is excited, but there are far too many indications of fear for us to pursue this type of play. There are so many exciting, non-fear eliciting ways to play – why choose this one? We need to look at the individual and work out whether this type of play is appropriate for that dog, in that situation, at that time, and for that dog's lifestyle. We need to read his body language to find out if he is enjoying the play, tolerating it, or is downright worried by it.

We also need to consider whether it would be better to play at a lower level of arousal before revving it up to high arousal. If the dog is highly aroused, is he able to switch off once the game is over? For dogs who cope confidently with rough play, this will not be an issue. For dogs who experience some element of fear when they are playing, it is more difficult; their adrenaline levels have rocketed and it will take far longer for them to return to a calm state. In this situation, you are venturing into a danger area, which could have unforeseen consequences. However, it would be sad for our dogs – and for our relationship with our dogs – if we banned all forms of contact or high-energy play just in case an element of fear crept in. But we do need to be constantly vigilant to ensure that play remains at acceptable levels of arousal, and that the dog is not rehearsing the emotion of fear while interacting with us.

HE WON'T PLAY WITH ME

Sometimes a dog appears to be very reluctant to play and owners give up saying: "he just won't play with me". Obviously this is not the end of the world but you are missing out on an important part of the special relationship you can have with your dog, and you are also losing a very useful training tool.

A dog who does not want to play will very often be the second dog in a family. He finds a readymade playmate in the well-established resident dog and will focus on him. He finds communication with the other dog so much more straightforward than it is with his human family so, understandably, he goes for the easy option. It may be that you try to play with the youngster only to be interrupted by the older dog who wants to join in. The young puppy quickly abandons playing with you in favour of the older dog, or if he continues to play he will be distracted, constantly checking to see what the other dog is doing.

Often the older dog takes over the toy; the youngster becomes so accustomed to giving up that he will rarely play if another dog is around. He therefore misses the opportunity of learning how to enjoy play with people. For working breeds, such as Collies, there is very little you need to do to increase play arousal and, therefore, it is easy to use as a reward in training or work situations. Other breeds – and individuals – may need to be stimulated to a much higher level

The Great Dane invites a game coming right into her playmate with an open, redirected, soft mouth.

Though her eyes and mouth look quite relaxed, her ear-set might suggest some apprehension.

Now she is under no pressure.

before they realise that humans are fun to play with. In this situation, a gentle tug on a toy, or running away a few paces in a mock chase, is not going to work. You need to involve the dog, making the toy come alive, but not overwhelming him, in order to get his commitment.

Every dog has the potential to play, but it can get lost quite easily. A classic example is when a young dog picks up something that he is not allowed to have; he is constantly told off and the item is taken away. As far as the youngster is concerned, there is no difference between a toy and a non-toy; he does not understand why he is being reprimanded and so he becomes increasingly anxious. Every time he has something in his mouth, he worries he may get told off, and the 'toy' may well be removed. His desire to play, and interact with his owner, becomes swiftly eroded.

This dog perceives she is being threatened by her owners, but she may not make the connection as to why. This could escalate into a defensive display.

DOG LED PLAY

How can you resist it when your dog invites you to play?

- "I've dropped the toy at your feet, wouldn't you like to throw it?"
- "Let's play tug with this rope."
- Or the very measured stance or play bow that pre-empts a highly exciting game of "catch me if you can!"

We feel so honoured when our dogs do the inviting. They want us humans, to play with them – even with our clumsy movements, lack of speed, even with the height and stance difference – they still want us to play. We are keen to respond. For a moment we get the chance, by invitation no less, to enter their world of fun and games. Fleetingly, we have assumed the role of honorary dog and we can communicate 'dog to dog'.

The games that dogs initiate take the form of toy-based invitations, where the dog drops the toy at your feet or shoves it into your hand asking you to interact with him. He may prefer to play on his own terms, dropping the toy just out of reach and grabbing it before you can get it. Or he may be the type that prefers chasing games.

The play bow, with forward ears and soft mouth, are a clear invitation to engage in fun.

All these games are accompanied by ritualised body language, which you soon learn to recognise. These games constitute quality time spent with your dog, but beware of the games that get out of hand. Mouthing can become part of a dog's play repertoire. The adult dog that tries to initiate this sort of play has either been encouraged by his owners responding in kind, or has been discouraged from play biting as a youngster but not been given an alternative outlet for his need to mouth something. Behaviourists are frequently called out to deal with this when it becomes a problem beyond puppyhood.

It may have started as intended play by the dog, but as his owners changed their response – perhaps telling off or angrily pushing him away – he becomes increasingly confused and elements of aggression begin to slip in.

If you play in this way, it is crucial you observe your dog's body language and, if anyone else in the family has said: "he doesn't like it", they will be right. They have observed some of those fear or avoiding communication signals. (See Rough-housing: Does your dog really want it? page 47).

However, if your dog mouths you in play and the

Walking in a curve around the toddler with head lowered, wide eyes not engaging the youngster, and furrowed brow – this is certainly not an invitation to play.

play is slow, often taking place with the dog lying in a relaxed position, with tail and facial features without any tension, and the mouth hardly closing, you have a dog that is enjoying the interaction and trusts you implicitly. You should feel honoured.

PLAY AND AROUSAL

If you respond to almost every play request your dog makes, you are in danger of over-doing it. For some dogs, particularly working dogs, this is very easy to do. In order to assess if it is too much for your dog, you need to understand how he is feeling during the play and the likely consequences as well. If your dog is worried about people – barking, appearing tense or using avoidance tactics – you need to reconsider what you are doing. Playing games that are highly arousing, based on fight and flight principles (which includes most non-toy games), will only serve to reinforce his suspicion and encourage him to mount a challenge when he meets people.

Over-exercised dogs get fitter and fitter and have greater and greater exercise needs, likewise dogs that are often described as hyperactive, but dogs that are played with excessively simply increase their play desire, and want to play at every possible opportunity. Play changes the fine biochemistry in both brain and body; the feel-good factor is undeniable but, when over-done, there are consequences. This happens easily when a 'working-bred' dog, with well-intentioned owners, slips into this vicious circle. Not only is his ability to settle and relax compromised, more significantly, his general, on-going arousal level is also affected. He then gets labelled as hyperactive!

If you have a dog that struggles to switch off, there are various strategies you can adopt:

- Practise exploratory sniffing, not playing, on walks.
- Limit the game to 4-6 throws at a time.
- Provide many more searches than chases.
- Use a toy that lands 'dead' and doesn't roll or bounce.
- Only play in specific areas, e.g. the hallway, or by a particular tree.

When you are working on these strategies, use a new toy which will help you to make these new associations.

For the dog who knows all about playing with you, it is easy to switch his focus into play as a means of avoiding a potential problem. If your dog becomes mildly stressed, or worried, you can use appropriate play before a problem develops. A bad experience will be more quickly forgotten with a fun game where your dog gives 100 per cent focus.

OUR UNINTENDED INVITATIONS

- "He wants to play all day"
- "He won't settle"
- "He never closes his eyes"
- "He never gives me any peace"
- "I've tried ignoring him but he just keeps on and on"

If you feel that one of the above statements, or something similar, applies to you and your dog, you should first be congratulated! You are clearly well tuned into the communication your dog uses to express what he wants. Many dog owners – sometimes even those who have had dogs all their lives, or train their dogs to quite a high standard – cannot or do not read their dogs well enough to know what they want. However just because your dog wants, does not mean he should get. You probably don't realise how much, and how often, you are the one effectively asking him: "What do you want?" How much are you encouraging him to be demanding or over active? How difficult are you making it for him to switch off and settle down?

Quite unintentionally, you may be inviting him to be a nuisance – many, many times a day – and this is most often done via eye contact. How much, and when, you give your dog eye contact has a huge impact on his behaviour. In its extreme it can make the difference between a pest and an angel; a dog described as hyperactive and a relaxed dog; a dog labelled neurotic and a chilled dog. You therefore owe it to your dog to be aware of when you give eye contact, and to avoid doing it when you are not wanting a response from him.

INVITING EYES

When you are interacting person to person, you rarely give eye contact unless you want to engage in conversation, yet you will make direct eye contact with your dog and expect him to make no response. An older, wiser dog may look sweetly back at you, but the majority of dogs expect this contact to lead to some form of activity. So you have created a situation where you have no intention of interacting with your dog, but he thinks: "you're looking at me, you're obviously inviting me to interact". For the dog obsessed with playing, it's is not the fact that you say: "just once more", or "that's enough now" that tells him the play session is at an end, it's because you break eye contact and look away. If you continue to look at your dog or even glance back at him, he won't believe you. For a dog, that look or glance is obviously an invitation. A dog that wanted to end a game or communication with another dog would never initiate eye contact. So when you want your dog to settle down, don't look at him. This also applies to looking at the toy – well, looking at the toy always precedes reaching down to get it, so you might just throw it... Your dog is a determined optimist.

These unintended invitations need managing if you have a demanding dog. You might be trying to send the right message when you ignore your dog if he barks for food or treats or for his toy to be thrown. But from the dog's perspective, it only takes a brief look in his direction and his hopes are sky high. He is also watching your body; the slightest move in the desired direction, which could be no more than a glance or a hand gesture, will raise his hopes. He doesn't see you as ignoring him; he just learns to watch you even more intently, waiting for that minute indication that you may respond. Once his hopes soar, your efforts to ignore him are in vain.

A dog is expert at picking up cues for the things that matter to him. He is quick to attach meaning within a split second, but he is slow to take account of other factors. His limited ability to reason means that it is only after numerous experiences of 'disappointment' that he learns, for example, that when you walk in the direction of a toy on a shelf, it does not necessarily

mean a game will follow. A careless look towards him will reawaken his expectations. When you take this on board, you realise why your actions are so easily misinterpreted, and it follows that you need to be hyper aware of where you are looking if you want the message to be clear for your dog.

SUMMING UP

Through the process of domestication, most of our pet dogs retain their juvenile attitude right through adulthood. Given the opportunity, our dogs love to play with us. Such play involves a two-way communication that strengthens the bond between the play partners. It can be used as a tool for practising self-control and adjusting arousal levels, for channelling focus and, of course, as a way to reward desirable behaviours. Play is a gift you can give to your dog.

The softness and lack of tension in the dog's body language, and a chase that is not happening at top speed, is unusual in a dog-human chase game. It tells us how confident and comfortable the dog is playing this game. What a trusting play relationship these two have.

Chapter Five

SPACE INVADERS

The issues of personal space

When a dog joins the family circle, he is a dependent being. He relies on his human family to provide food and shelter and to safeguard his health. The domesticated dog has evolved from his wolf ancestors, but he no longer needs to be part of a pack to survive. His priorities have changed and people have become of prime importance. If a puppy comes from a well socialised litter there is hardly a moment when people do not matter. The puppies' mother is the initial source of food and comfort, but from the instant a new pup is touched and maybe picked up by the breeder, he is engaging with another species, starting a relationship which is of supreme significance.

For some puppies, human providers are nothing but good news. The bold, extrovert puppy is happy to be handled, quick to pick up on human signals which tell him something good is happening, such as the arrival of food, and is ready to seek out interactions in the form of play. However, there are some puppies who struggle with incursions into their personal space. This may be related to breed type or their own particular bloodlines. But it can also be learnt from observing their mother's adverse reactions or as a result of poor socialisation where exposure to new people and situations has been limited or negative. So when you bring a puppy into your home, you are not dealing with an entirely clean slate. An adult dog has even more history but, with tact and understanding, you can reduce or even overcome any anxieties he might have.

HANDLING

Intolerance to being handled is something that cannot be ignored. Throughout his life, a dog needs to be touched and moved. He needs routine care in the form of flea treatment and nail trimming, and if he is long-coated, he will need regular grooming. There will be occasions when he has to be examined by you, or a vet, and undergo treatment, and there will be times when you simply need to move him from one place to another.

Your job is to make these procedures as comfortable for your dog as possible. You need to read his body language and pick up on the signals showing

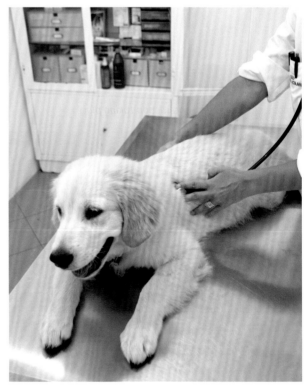

Although this puppy doesn't look his happiest – ears in, tight lips – he's certainly not in freeze mode. Neither is he thinking about trying to escape, indicated by his spread elbows. He is not overwhelmed by the situation.

you what he is finding difficult. In this way, you can adapt your handling to be more sympathetic so that he never feels the need to escalate his behaviour. Many first bite incidents occur when a dog is being examined by a vet, which is a damning reflection on our lack of preparation, and the miscommunication, which has led him to such an extreme measure.

With regular handling most puppies learn to be calm and still during invasive interactions with their human family. This is certainly made easier if the breeder has worked on moving the pups, weighing them, examining them, trimming nails and maybe even grooming them. But what should you do if your puppy or adult dog is either fearful or resentful when you handle him? The first step is to tune into his body language so you can understand what he is feeling.

The held back ears and wide eyes show this dog is feeling apprehensive about the interaction taking place.

These clues are not being heeded, so he turns his head away trying to avert what he regards as a potential threat.

Dogs who struggle with this form of attention can generally be divided into two categories: those that freeze and/or roll over, and those that squirm, wriggle

LESSONS IN RELAXATION

Helping Out

The priority is to help your dog to feel better about being handled. As he starts to relax you will see his body and facial features loosening up.

Only at this point should you use treats to reward the outward, physical behaviour. If you use treats to elicit the behaviour you want, your dog may comply but he will still be showing signs that he feels threatened or under pressure.

Nail trimming is often viewed as an ordeal by dog and owner alike – but it doesn't have to be that way.

and mouth you. In most cases, the behaviour will be more extreme in puppies; an adult dog may have developed coping strategies but his concerns will still be apparent.

FREEZE AND ROLL OVER

If your dog is the type that freezes and possibly goes as far as rolling over when he is being handled, you will probably notice a stilling as you begin to handle him. He may show an upright stiffness before rolling over, but he is more likely to lower his posture, shrinking his body into his elbows. He puts up no kind of a struggle so you may be misled into thinking that he is being good. However, you need to look at the body language; this seemingly compliant behaviour masks a major lack of confidence.

His strategy is to dissuade you from threatening him – because that is how he perceives your intervention. If a puppy or a youngster was approached by a scary dog, you would see the same body language. His avoidance

ROLL OVERS

It is clear that this youngster is not asking for a tummy tickle. He perceives what is about to happen could be unpleasant.

We need to know:
- The dog's usual pattern of behaviour
- Observe muscle tension/relaxation
- Be on the look out for avoidance behaviours beforehand or relief behaviours after the interaction (shake off, fast movement on getting up or zoomies).

These dogs are making it clear how they feel:

A roll over was used to placate the woman. It didn't work so the dog is forced into becoming defensive.

"I love you, I love you – but this is so strange."

"PLEASE don't move me."

So we should not presume that these dogs are asking for a tummy rub:

"Ah, bliss! Pure bliss!"

"I'm only little, honestly I'm no threat to you."

behaviour may seem mild and unimportant at this stage but, if ignored, it can become increasingly proactive. By the time the dog is six or seven months, he may even be using aggressive displays to defend himself. Interestingly, the Spaniel breeds seem to specialise in rolling over when they are resisting handling. It is generally a quick roll over; initially the head is held in and the tail is tucked between the legs. As with the dog that freezes, this is a clear sign that the individual needs a boost to his confidence.

It will help if you take a step or two back from him, giving a clear signal that you are not posing a threat. This will reduce his level of stress; he will then get up to move towards you so you can reward him when he is on four feet again. It is a good plan to teach him to stand and use treats so you can pre-empt the roll over. This type of dog needs be handled on a regular basis, but sessions should be of very short duration to minimise the pressure he is experiencing. Choose an environment that is familiar, calm and free from distractions, and choose times when he is relaxed.

It is very tempting to call your dog to you when you want to start a handling session, backing it up with lots of encouragement. But while he is unsure about being handled, this can build a negative association with his name and with the recall. Instead, approach him quietly and handle him with the minimum of fuss. Make sure you only give treats when he is showing more relaxed body language, loosening up rather than freezing, standing on four feet rather than rolling over. Be aware that luring with a treat may get the behaviour you want, e.g. a stand rather than a roll over, but it may be masking the emotion of fear. Read your dog's body language so you are only reinforcing increases in confidence.

WRIGGLERS AND SQUIRMERS

The dog who wriggles and squirms when being handled – and sometimes even air snaps – has often learnt this behaviour as a puppy after being carelessly handled, especially by children. When a puppy wriggles, he often escapes or is put down very abruptly which, of course, reinforces his urge to struggle when he is being restrained. You can counter this by only putting him down – as that is what he wants – as a reward for brief moments of stillness. This type of reaction can very easily develop into a frustrated, aggressive

display and needs careful handling. You can usually detect the change from play or minor resistance to aggression by the speed of reactions. A dog that has no aggressive intent will do everything – the wriggling, the squirming, the mouthing – at a much slower pace. A speed increase is often the first indication that the behaviour is tipping towards aggression.

BREAK OFF IF HE GROWLS

While you want to be sensitive to what your dog likes or dislikes, there will always be things, such as ear cleaning or feet drying, that need to be done so the dog must learn a reasonable degree of tolerance and acceptance. Teaching a dog to accept restraint and treatment should be done gradually, so that he never feels provoked to make an aggressive signal. In this way we make good associations with being handled prior to the dog being in pain or treatment being necessary. He should be so used to you handling and touching him sensitively that when, out of necessity, it does hurt him, he doesn't blame it on you or your handling.

If he does give a warning growl, do not ignore it, or verbally or physically correct him, as this allows him no room to manoeuvre. If he is left without a choice he has no option but to move on to the next stage and escalate his behaviour into actual aggression. You want your dog to accept what you are doing to him, but you do not want him to believe that growling doesn't work. A dog that gives no warning is a much more dangerous animal. If you handle your dog regularly, encouraging and rewarding the behaviour you want, you should never get to the growling stage. If he does growl at that particular moment, back away. But see it as a warning and get to work on a confidence-building programme without delay.

Take heed of lip quivers even if there is no growl.

56 MEASURES TO HELP YOUR DOG

There are a number of ways to help your dog feel more comfortable with being handled and groomed, which although minor in themselves, can make a big difference to the way he feels – and reacts. The effort it takes is minimal in comparison to the emotional stress you can spare him.

The Jack Russell's head duck suggests a degree of avoidance, but the lack of tension in the neck and facial features portrays the trust that has been built up over time in his young owner.

- Practise restraint and handling when your dog is not sore or in pain so he has a solid foundation of pleasant experiences.
- Become familiar with the way his body works in terms of moving his limbs. This will mean that you can handle him sympathetically.
- Give yourself time or it leads to compromising the dog's comfort and hence, his trust.
- Remove or change anything that is perceived as a threat. Is there something about you, your grooming tools, or where you have positioned him, that is causing concern?
- Is there something in the environment that is concerning him? Does he feel threatened by the presence of other dogs, children, or the family cat?
- Be aware of areas where he might be ticklish or over-sensitive, or where he is experiencing pain or discomfort.
- Dilute the more difficult areas of handling/ grooming/drying by working predominantly in areas where your dog likes to be touched or stroked. If your dog lets you know he is feeling under pressure, stop what you are doing. Allow him to move away,

WHEN YOU JUST HAVE TO DO IT

- Distract so your dog's focus is elsewhere.
- Get ready to go for a walk and carry out the handling procedure with the front door ajar.
- Scratch or give a deep massage elsewhere on his body.
- Be generous with novel, tasty treats or smeared paste
- Do something interesting and active immediately before and immediately afterwards.
- Get on with it so he has no time to anticipate and build up negative expectation.
- Discreetly get everything prepared beforehand.
- Don't recall him or ask him to come.
- Aim for a mild surprise – but not when he's resting.
- Be quick and calm.

- While the Beagle is being distracted by the father, a thorn or perhaps a tick is removed. The Beagle's posture tell us he is relaxed about this handling. His head is up, his rear end is in a semi lying down posture, his back is curved in the opposite way to that of a tense dog trying to avoid a situation. He is also leaning into, not away from the person examining him. His tail carriage, the tension in his front right leg, the facial tension and focus towards the father suggest he is anticipating a treat.

but take note so that you are more sensitive next time.

- Be aware that the way in which you touch and move your dog may be easily misinterpreted, even though you don't intend any threat. Leaning over him, dragging him, moving him by his scruff, staring straight at him while cleaning his eyes or trimming his face, touching or examining his penis or anus area – all are open to misinterpretation. Attend to these difficult areas in brief bursts, spending much more time on areas he is comfortable with.

- When moving your dog by his collar, use calm, non-threatening body language, and do not jerk or pull him. Instead, take hold of his collar and wait for him to move in the direction of your gently applied pressure. Turn your shoulders, hips and eyes in the direction you wish your dog to go to make easily read signposts.

The continuing use of praise, reassurance, and treats while you are handling in a way that your dog perceives as threatening carries a risk. He may well form a negative association, thus devaluing, or even poisoning, your intended rewards.

LET SLEEPING DOGS LIE

This is an old adage and many cultures have similar sayings. Perhaps it is reassuring to acknowledge that dogs all over the world don't like being disturbed when they are half asleep or sleeping. We respect our fellow humans' right to rest without being disturbed but, for some reason, we do not apply this to the family dog. We are all guilty of giving attention to a dog when we feel like it, regardless of whether the dog appreciates it.

This is especially true of children who struggle to understand that a dog needs down time and space. Instead of accusing the dog of being bad-tempered if he struggles in this situation, we should look out for the early signs which show he is uncomfortable: stilling, licking lips, yawning, turning away, perhaps wide-eyed or following the child's movement without moving his head. Hopefully you, and your children, will read the subtle signals so your dog never feels he has to put up with unwanted attention or feels the need to move away.

The stiffness of this dog as she tries to turn away, while still keeping an eye on the toddler and his hand tells of her unease.

Wanting to settle in peace, without being touched, leads to this Dalmatian turning his head away with closely held ears. Adults need to help children see and respect what their dogs are saying.

Even though this young boy is moving, the Labrador's confidence is evident by the relaxed, heavy head.

Tragically, there are far too many instances of a child's face being bitten and sometimes disfigured when they have tried to cuddle their own or a friend's normally sociable dog. These incidents are preventable. The dog in question would have previously shown freezing, appeasing, avoidance or defensive behaviours indicating his dislike of being disturbed and/or being cuddled – if only we would listen.

Unfortunately, it is all too easy to ignore or be unaware of the pre-aggressive signals given off by a polite dog. He is giving clear indications of his unease but because he is using body language that is a step below a growl or snarl, it is not taken seriously enough to prompt bite prevention action. Just like people, there will be some dogs who don't appear to mind being disturbed as much as others. A few just sleep through it, maintaining soft sleep body language, but they are in the minority. The only way to monitor reactions is by watching the individual dog. Don't kid yourself; behaviour such as rolling over, sitting up and giving you kisses back are to appease and calm you – it doesn't mean your dog likes it. Dogs that have gone on to growl, snap and bite will have used these behaviours in the early stages. Although a progression to aggressive behaviour is not inevitable, it confirms that appeasing behaviour, and even mild avoidance behaviours, should send out strong signals which need to be heeded.

RESTING PLACES

During the course of a day, a dog may settle to rest as many as 30 times, and he may choose any of 10 or so different places to settle in. Sometimes the choice is linked to comfort - soft and warm in front of the fire or radiator, soft and supportive for tired or sore limbs, hard and cool for hot dogs or when just back from a walk. Comfort is a major consideration, but settling somewhere that is heavily scented of you is just as desirable. Your bed or your lounge chair smell great; the dirty laundry pile also makes a luxurious, highly desirable place to snooze. It may not be your choice, but your dog knows what he likes. A look-out sentry is a common choice for dogs who enjoy guarding. Being able to see outside and catnap at the same time is a sought-after position – on top of sofas, halfway up the stairs, or within sight of the front door – all make

desirable posts for the alarm dog (which may not be such a good thing!).

Look-out sentries are also selected by the dog who wants to keep half an eye on his family – doorways, bottom of the stairs, or any other vantage point where he can see all the important comings and goings of his family – where he can settle without having to continuously get up or check where everyone is, and what is happening. Dogs like den-type places. These are often chosen when a dog wants to settle in peace – under the table, in the corner, behind the settee. In all likelihood, he needs a place where there is a reduction in the visual and auditory stimulation, making it easier for him to switch off. Dogs that are frightened will often seek out den-type areas, too; it can be a great support for a dog worried by fireworks or thunder to have a den that minimises sound and light. In this situation a dog will often try to dig deeper and bury himself, and this may include scrabbling at your mattress stuffing, or all the junk you had forgotten about in an under-stairs cupboard.

A dog may seek out a vantage point where he can view the family's comings and goings.

TWO'S COMPANY

Sleeping on your lap, half on half off you, snoozing with his head on your feet, or just alongside you is a highly sought-after place for most dogs. A dog will tolerate a lot of other not-so-pleasant factors just to have that physical contact with his human. This is a bonding experience for both of you. However, there are a large number of dogs that don't want, or don't seek this contact. For some breeds and types this is fairly normal; there may be a genetic element involved in their preference for physical independence, or it may date back to something that happened in puppyhood. In some situations, your dog may feel that it's just not the right time for relaxing.

Whatever the reason, if your dog is not comfortable settling in physical contact with you – if when you invite him he turns his head or walks away, if he licks his lips, or goes into hyper-busy mode – let him be. Don't force yourself on him or make him come and lie beside you – he won't enjoy it and he cannot understand what you are doing.

THREE'S A CROWD

There are dogs who do not want to be approached when they are settled by themselves. Some of these also dislike being approached when they are settled on, or with you. They don't want a third person or another dog. Going still, staring fixedly at the 'intruder', moaning, or even growling and air snapping – these are often linked to the anticipation of being made or told to "get off" or "move over". In this situation the dog regards you as a resource; perceives the approaching person as a threat to what he wants – staying in close physical contact with you. Seen from his perspective, those fears are justified if you reprimand him or tell him to move away. Typically a vicious circle develops leading to an escalation in the warning signals displayed. However if you are tactful – getting up with him, for example – he does not need to feel his favourite place is being compromised.

CAN'T POSSIBLY MOVE

Something funny happens when a dog settles somewhere, in fact when he settles anywhere - he cannot possibly move. It is almost as if even if he wanted to move, he just cannot. Once lying down, no matter how much he dislikes what is happening – the baby about to crawl on him, the toddler about to hug him, you about to kiss him – he doesn't seem to be able to move away.

It would seem obvious to us, but it seems to rarely be in the canine repertoire. This 'stickiness' often leads to conflict but if you observe your dog's communication, it need not escalate into a problem. If he is going into a freeze, turning away, licking

or yawning, or giving you his tummy, call him to something – anything – rather than go into his space. Avoid taking his collar and pulling him as this can easily be perceived as threatening. Finding a way of calling him to you so he gets off the seat or bed is potentially far less challenging. Enjoy watching your dog make choices of where and when he settles. Enjoy his contact if he offers it, but also be prepared to enjoy letting him have his own space if that is his preferred pleasure. Only then will be able to chase rabbits in his sleep…

Too tired? Unwell? Wanting peace?

DOGS UNDER PRESSURE

Today's dog can have a very busy schedule, particularly if he is involved in some form of specialist training or competitive activity. There may be group training sessions, one-on-one training, trips to the vet, the groomer, the physiotherapist, as well as the routine outings to the local park with you or a dog walker. In addition there may be one-offs, such as going on holiday and being put into boarding kennels or day care.

A growing trend in dog ownership is the increasing number of different people who may handle your dog, and the variety of places and establishments he may visit in his lifetime. There are dogs who relish these experiences, embracing the novelty. They are keen to meet all these different people; ready to be wooed by treats, the opportunity to meet other dogs or to sniff out evidence of their earlier presence. There are many who settle into a busy diary of engagements and are ready to enjoy the familiarity of that routine unfolding. For other dogs, however, this schedule involves a degree of pressure that, given the choice, they would avoid.

How your dog copes with these situations depends largely on three factors:

- Your dog's personality
- How he is handled
- Past experiences

YOUR DOG'S PERSONALITY

Each dog is an individual with his own unique personality, and while there are similar traits within breeds and within breeding lines, there is a lot of individuality, too. The robust, confident dog who enjoys novelty will cope well, and may not even find these situations challenging. The sensitive dog, who is shy or nervous and who struggles with novelty is the other extreme. For him, these situations are perceived as threatening. Who handles him and how he is handled will have far reaching implications.

HOW HE IS HANDLED ...and by whom

In some of these situations you will be present, perhaps holding, positioning and moving your dog. Most dogs will be more comfortable with this; the familiarity is helpful and gives us a concrete way to prepare the dog for the varied experiences he may be exposed to. However, it is inevitable that your dog will come across professionals who are vastly different in appearance, voice, smell, and in the way they move and handle him, and so he will feel unprepared.

In the same way, we humans feel more anxious when we encounter people who are not in our regular, daily circle. We are not as comfortable with differences until they become familiar – but that ease and familiarity can only be achieved with time. For your dog, the body language used by a relative stranger is highly significant. A professional with a calm, relaxed way of moving, handling and talking is clearly less intimidating. Professionals who are careful to avoid movements and gestures that could be misinterpreted by a dog, such as facial stares, moving directly towards the dog's face, bending over the top of the dog, or fast or rough handling, – are less likely to be perceived as threatening. The professional can only be sensitive to the extent he can read your dog. He will be observing:

- Level of pain or discomfort the dog is experiencing.

- How long the dog will tolerate examination/ manipulation.

As each dog is so different it can take considerable time for the less experienced professional to tune into an individual's limits. They may only realise them when they step very close to the threshold. However, sensitive and communication-aware professionals become astonishingly competent at working below this threshold.

PAST EXPERIENCES

The first time many dogs show aggression is when being handled by a vet or a groomer. This will be strongly linked to previous experiences and can have a profound effect on future encounters. As already highlighted, a dog that is used to being handled – having his tail lifted up, or someone looking down his ears – will be much less concerned than the dog who experiences it for the first time with a professional. Therefore, accustoming your dog to this somewhat invasive attention, which might be employed by a vet or a groomer, is an important life skill to learn. If you do this with sensitivity, using your ability to read your dog's emotional state and gradually building up the level of handling, you can reduce potential stress to a minimum.

A bad experience can have long lasting implications.

However, previous experiences with that professional, in that venue, or with that type of handling, will be stored in your dog's memory. The more traumatic he found the experience, the deeper it will be ingrained, and therefore his stress levels will be quick to resurface. It is less about what happened

TEACHING ACCEPTANCE OF HANDLING

Helping Out

- Initially choose times when you are both calm and relaxed.
- Progress at your dog's pace, i.e. sufficiently slow so that he does not feel tense enough to move away, lip-lick or use a calming/displacement signal.
- Hold him gently for two seconds, giving him treats at the same time, and then release him.
- Gradually increase the time you are restraining him, while constantly giving treats.
- When he is not being held, he gets no treats.

PROVIDING HE IS RELAXED ABOUT THIS HANDLING:

- When you start handling, allow a slight delay before you begin giving treats.
- If that goes well, reduce to occasional treats during handling, but treat well the moment you finish.
- Be in tune with your dog, start off with the handling procedure that is easiest for him.
- Prioritising your dog's emotional progress may mean you need to go excruciatingly slowly. Celebrate every little step forward.
- Build up to handling in more sensitive areas.
- Gradually change times and places for your handling session and, in time, allow other members of the family to take part.

on a particular occasion, but all about how your dog perceived it. If he felt frightened or threatened, the damage has been done. This puts a huge onus on us to change his perception. We need to:

- Prepare him for all sorts of handling so he is comfortable with this type of attention from those outside his immediate family circle.
- Make sure the professional you employ is sensitive and is prepared to take time to get to know your dog.

Undoing the damage and rebuilding confidence is almost impossible with deeply traumatised dogs. But with severely affected dogs – and with a great deal of hard work – you can make useful progress.

MONITORING REACTIONS

Unfortunately it is how a dog reacts rather than how he feels which will influence the way he is treated. This is why it is imperative to train your dog to accept handling before entrusting him to professionals who do not always have the time, or the sensitivity, to ameliorate a tense situation.

Though not aggressive, this dog is certainly not enjoying being groomed. In a tense, upright position, with ears pinned back and tight lips, he tips his hips away and thrusts his head towards the groomer's hand, following its movement. The initial part of this move is similar to a bite movement – another dog would back away from this level of warning.

Although this is not quite a submissive roll over, this Husky flops backwards and attempts to turn the situation into play by mouthing. The intention is to evade the process in a completely non-aggressive way – what a great dog!

If your dog is feeling under pressure he will generally respond in one of four ways; in human and mammalian psychology these are commonly termed the 4Fs:

- Fight
- Flight
- Freeze
- Faff (frolic and fool around)

If your dog opts for the fight or flight mode, his reaction will be fairly obvious, and what credit to our domesticated dogs that most of the 'fight' dogs will give early clues and if not forced further, will avoid the fight element. Unless a dog has previously been pushed into being aggressive, he will rarely bite without prior warning. There will be early signs that he is uncomfortable – yawning, licking, head turning, wide eyes, a freeze or tense stillness.

Be very aware of his mouth: was he panting and now holding his mouth closed? Check the tension of his cheeks and lips; any slight quiver or lift of lips, or a grumble presents an opportunity for you to back down and select an alternative approach. If ignored, your dog will perceive the threat as escalating and will respond accordingly. He will also have learnt that his warnings are ineffective so there is a good chance that he will omit them, or increase them, the next time he feels threatened.

However if his warnings are heeded, he will not feel the need to escalate his behaviour to bite level. This is the lifeline that all dogs should be offered – a dog that warns need never bite.

PROFESSIONALS UNDER PRESSURE

Ideally professionals who handle dogs would have an understanding of dog psychology and body language but, all too often, it is constraint of time that causes the biggest problems. If a professional does not have time to take on board your dog's individuality, what chance do they have of administering sympathetic treatment? Obviously you need to give as much information as possible if your dog has even the slightest tendency to be aggressive in these situations, but you must also do what you can to avoid unnecessary and possibly damaging time constraints.

Do not go for an appointment where your dog is being squeezed in. The groomer in a hurry to detangle a coat, the dog walker rushing to get your dog in or out of the van, the kennel staff already behind time with a hundred other jobs, or the exhausted vet with a waiting room full of patients - they cannot possibly find the time to be sensitive to a struggling dog.

If your dog is the inhibited type, he may freeze or go relatively still in a stand, sit or a down. As a strategy, this is positively useful for the professional that is involved in handling, manipulating or giving treatment to your dog. The lack of movement and passive compliance make it so much easier and, even though an inhibited dog is less likely to give information about where and when it hurts, he does not pose a risk and can be dealt with quickly and efficiently. But this inhibited behaviour is caused by fear, which could be as great, or even greater, than in the dog that uses a defensive display.

If you see this type of inhibited behaviour in your dog, you need to guard against subjecting him to over frequent or unnecessary treatment just because he is "no trouble". You cannot explain to him that you are doing it because:

- It will make him feel better
- It's good for him
- He will look so much better
- It just has to be done

You can provide the justification, but your dog cannot understand why he is being put through an ordeal which he finds both threatening and frightening. Whether you have a seemingly well-behaved dog or a dog that might be pushed to an aggressive reaction, you should minimise handling by others while building up resilience at home.

The worried dog that goes down the 'faff around' route is generally less stressed by handling. Yes, he can be a nuisance when he tries to 'kiss' (appease) everyone nearby, but this method of trying to resolve a frightening situation is generally associated with a quick recovery time and less reluctance than the flight/fight or freeze brigade to revisit the situation. It is therefore reasonable to conclude that the stress – and therefore the negative impact – is less, so you have much more choice in what it is reasonable to subject him to.

A DUMB ANIMAL LEFT IN PAIN

If a dog is in pain and we do nothing about it, it's a welfare issue, isn't it? But, if a dog is in pain, and we don't even recognise it, is it still a welfare issue? Ignorance may be hurting your dog. Vets, well-educated behaviourists and trainers so often come across dogs that are experiencing pain but the owner isn't recognising it. Why does this happen?

At the core of this issue is the clash between human and canine communication. Our human nature says: "he isn't crying so he can't be in pain" or "he chases the ball so he can't be in pain". Canine nature says: "there's dinner/a sheep/a rat running away - get it!" So that's what he does, and even if he feels pain, his survival instincts says: "don't show pain or injury, it makes you vulnerable". For your dog's wellbeing you need to read his body language so that you recognise signs of pain, and then take the appropriate action.

COPING WITH PAIN

Pain is a very complicated topic; it is extremely subjective. What I find painful you may not; what is painful when I move one way, may not be when I move differently; when I'm watching my favourite TV programme I may not even be aware of the pain. It is all about how you feel it, which is not very useful if you don't know how your dog feels. But, in fact, there is no one better than you – the owner – to judge how your dog feels.

No vet has as much access to information as you have about whether your dog is in pain, and to what extent. You are the ultimate judge of what is different about your dog. Only you know if he's quieter, more unsettled, withdrawn, sleeping or drinking more, standing, reticent about moving or lying in a position that's unusual for him. You are the best person to notice an increase in sensitivity or ticklishness and to know that he's not usually reluctant to jump in the car, or that he now takes longer to stand up. You are the judge of his pain, you are his spokesperson; the vet can then be the doctor.

Humans have very different levels of pain sensitivity. Dogs are no different; there are differences in pain thresholds between breeds, types of dogs and individuals. No self-respecting Great Dane, Dobermann or Pomeranian would go hell-for-leather through what looks like an impenetrable thicket of

OFTEN MISSED INDICATORS OF PAIN

A dog will show obvious signs of discomfort, but the vigilant owners should be aware of other signs that indicate all is not well:

- Sudden onset of grumpiness or aggression.
- Difficulty settling – pacing/fidgety/frequent re-positioning.
- Panting for 'no reason'.
- Ears almost permanently held back.
- Taking longer to stand up and lie down.
- All over stiffness.
- Hesitancy or reluctance to respond to requests, e.g. jump in the car, sit or down.
- Unusual resistance to be being touched, handled, restrained, or towel-dried.

brambles, but to the Spaniels and Terriers, there is no such word as 'impenetrable'!

How much easier it is to train a physically sensitive Greyhound or Bedlington Terrier to walk on a lead without pulling, than to teach a Siberian Husky or a Gordon Setter, who appear to take a positive pleasure in bracing their shoulders and straining their necks as they attempt to force the pace.

A Whippet or Chinese Crested will do everything possible to avoid stepping on stones, but if you saw the same behaviour in a Mastiff or a Labrador, you would know that something was wrong. Selective breeding has also contributed to the differing pain thresholds. In the fighting breeds, individuals that showed heightened sensitivity would not be bred from. Conversely it may not matter if a lap dog is particularly sensitive to pain – a low pain threshold might even make it more endearing to our mothering needs.

A dog's desire to live life to the full can send the wrong messages. Pain can momentarily be put aside if a dog is highly motivated or distracted. The adrenaline that is pumping, and the drive to carry on overrides all else, albeit temporarily. You see this in ball-mad dogs and agility junkies; these dogs cannot resist the impulse to run, chase, hunt, track or herd. For many

The expression on this old girl's face is typical of a dog experiencing long-term discomfort:

- The eyes are alert and focused on her owner – or staring into the distance – but her head is not facing the same direction.

- Her body and her ears are directed backwards – this position can become an almost permanent state.

- Despite physical restrictions, her body and her facial features appear to be slumped.

pet dogs, play is the highlight of their daily life. It is what they live for so it takes a lot of pain to put them off. There are many stories of dogs that continued to follow their bicycling owner or play ball until they literally collapsed, or who carried on jumping an agility course despite a fractured leg. Pain is put on hold until the activity stops. It is only by reading your dog's behaviour and body language when he is not highly motivated that tells you about his pain. What he does when he is aroused tells you about his motivation, not his pain.

Every behaviour specialist knows a sudden, unexplained change in behaviour is likely to be linked to pain. It is the red flag. This is most commonly seen as aggressive and grumpy behaviour, but it can also be linked to behaviours like tail chasing and licking, and even to separation anxiety. In human terms, our ability to cope with daily tasks is affected when we are ill. In exactly the same way, the grumpy dog is letting you know that what you are doing to him, or asking him to do, no longer feels OK.

We can only do the best for our dogs if we listen to them. If we learn to listen to their whispers, they will never need to shout.

WHAT YOU CAN DO?

If your dog is poorly, in pain, or having to be moved, held or touched in a way that is isn't comfortable – unless we teach otherwise – your intervention will be perceived as threatening. However, sensitive handling and manipulation when your dog is well will negate you as the source of any later pain

If your dog growls, back away at that moment to prevent an aggressive reaction. Address the cause later. Remember, a dog that gives a warning growl will never bite unless we force him to it.

Set your dog up for success not stress. This is easy to achieve with proper planning, due consideration, and allocating sufficient time for the task required. A dog that is so scared he is inhibited, or freezes, is often ignorantly described as "tolerant" or "well-behaved" – watch out for this.

Bear in mind, pain and discomfort may not be shown when a dog is highly motivated – for example, during greeting, play and or when he is anticipating a walk or a meal. You, therefore, need to look out for clues at other times.

Don't ever forget, nobody knows your dog like you do – and you are his voice.

Chapter Six

UNINTENDED CONSEQUENCES

How unwanted behaviours develop

We humans have the biggest effect on how our dogs behave. For the most part this is a good thing but, sometimes, our actions have consequences we do not expect, often leading to stress and undesirable behaviour. There are times when we just get it wrong: we fail to see a situation from the dog's perspective, and the dog misunderstands our intentions.

THE POWER AND THE FALL-OUT OF ROUTINES

Routines become a way of communicating to the dog what will happen: when and in what order or sequence. This learnt predictability can be useful and oil the cogs of daily life. It can allow the dog to relax and settle in between the exciting daily events of feeding, playing, greeting family and walking. Knowing that X won't happen until Y has happened can be informative and reassuring, meaning the dog doesn't have to be in a constant state of anticipation. Patterns are easily learnt by dogs.

However, in households where every day has exactly the same pattern of times and events, this predictability can become problematic. The build up and excitement gets earlier and earlier as the dog works out what precedes the preceding events that precede the exciting event! They learn that the aroused or expectant behaviour – drooling, staring, pacing, whining, barking – can be a source of irritation to us humans, even though we created the pattern in the first place.

There can also be a fall-out for the dog that becomes stressed if the daily pattern is changed or has to be altered. This can be so severe that he won't eat, or can't settle because he hasn't had his walk at

Dogs are remarkably good at back-chaining events.

the appointed hour. If only you could tell him: "it's because I have to go for a dental appointment" or "your leg needs to be rested – the vet has banned you from walks for two weeks" or "you have diarrhoea – no treats!" It's important to be aware of how much a dog builds up his hopes or expectations within the routines that you create.

LET'S GO!

Going for a walk is the highspot of your dog's day and he is, understandably, keen to spot the signs that tell him you are getting ready to take him out. He is an expert in picking up clues: subtle and obvious, intentional and unintentional. You probably have no idea that you vaguely glanced in your dog's direction as you thought about his walk, but he will have noticed it long before you said: "Let's go!"

Some of the clues he picks up are closely linked; he waits for you to say "right" as you get up from

66

the chair, he looks out for your focused movement towards the shoe rack, and watches as you put your keys in your pocket. But the dog that has become accustomed to your routine is always trying to work out what the previous clues are to the link he already knows, so that he can add yet another link...The links will be made further and further back creating a long pattern string. For example, arrive home, greeting, let dog into garden, get changed, have a cup of tea, write emails, watch the news, put away the dishes, get ready to go for a walk. Same pattern day in, day out.

So starts any number of anticipatory behaviours; your dog may start whining and barking, which will often be high-pitched and orientated at you, he may start pacing or jump up at you, perhaps momentarily on and off you, he may try mouthing you or grabbing anything that comes to hand, or simply staring intently at you – all intended to communicate: "hurry up". It's usually successful as you want put a stop to his antics which, of course, acts as a highly relevant reward, strengthening and intensifying his behaviour.

The more you get annoyed, the more the dog becomes further aroused. Attempts to train him in this context by not attaching his lead until he sits, not opening the door until he's quiet, or reversing your direction if he pulls on the lead, may only serve to increase frustration. If your dog struggles with self-control when he's at a medium level of arousal, he will not be receptive, or be able to work things out, when he is at this level of excitement.

BEING LEFT BEHIND

The ability to chain events further and further backwards can have a devastating effect on anxious dogs who struggle to cope when they are left home alone. For a well-adjusted dog, the departure of his owner is a chance to have a well-earned rest; he may just stand and watch you leave, or maybe go to his settling place and lie down with a sigh. For other dogs, being left is a bit harder. This type of dog may observe the leaving clues with head and tail dropped, watching your every move, possibly standing and following, or maybe going to his resting place and lying down, but remaining very focused on you. He may watch and wait for a minute or so by the door or he may peer out of the window while you drive off.

SURPRISE, SURPRISE!

If you keep the pattern string short – making sure that getting ready to go out for a walk is the only reliable walk predictor – you will be are astonished at how much calmer the frustrated dog can be. If the period between knowing it's time for a walk to being on the street is seconds rather than minutes, his anticipatory behaviour is kept in check. You can therefore add in a brief stand still, or small move back from the door, progressing to a brief sit.

When your dog is too aroused, especially if there is frustration as well, he can hardly hear you; he struggles to process what you have said, and certainly won't find it easy to employ self-control. By condensing the time scale, you are creating a situation where your dog is still able to listen to you. So make it easy for him, and eventually for yourself. Surprise him to such an extent that you get perfect behaviours, which you will be rewarding with a walk, and if you take things gradually and consistently, the anticipatory behaviours will fade.

Once you are gone, he may check the house in case you haven't really gone, or he may be intent on seeing if you have left anything edible within his reach – he'll soon sort that out. Then resignation leads to relaxation and sleep. The dog coping well with being left can eat the chew or stuffed kong that you left for him. He shows evidence (if you sneak back) of having just woken up and appears rested on your return. He greets and is delighted to see you. He isn't panting, thirsty or stressed, and he quickly settles down after a minute or two of greeting. But for others, being left behind is much more traumatic.

A dog will pick up clues concerning arrivals and departures.

AVOIDING SEPARATION PROBLEMS

Initial separation should be done when the puppy or new dog has been fed, watered and is relaxed and ready to settle.

- Keep the drama out of your leaving cues and be casual on your return.
- Never, ever, tell your dog off when you return – no matter what he did in your absence.
- Address sound sensitivity issues, making sure you are not part of the answer (see page 68).

"PLEASE DON'T LEAVE ME"

Owners of dogs with separation problems sometimes get an additional dog in the hope that having company will make being left more bearable. This tactic is only, very occasionally, successful. For most dogs it is all about you. You are the source of food, walks, fun, comfort, but most importantly – relaxation. Dogs that are unable to relax may give you clues that this is the case – barking, toileting, destructive behaviour and complaints from neighbours are the obvious indicators.

However, there are many very anxious dogs that show none of these overt signs, but still display a number of telltale signals to look out for:

Eating

- Not being able to eat a chew or treat when left, but gobbling it on your return.
- Not being able to eat when he realises you are preparing to leave.
- Reduced appetite for a period of time following your return.

Tiredness

- When you return home he seems shattered. Finally he can relax, and he is probably very much in need of sleep.
- Inability to snooze, relax or even put his head down, when he is aware that you might be leaving at some stage.
- Any daytime sleep will be poor quality; he will be easily disturbed.

Panting/drooling

- He drinks lots of water when you are away.
- He fails to drink when you are away, but drinks copiously when you get back.
- He pants from the first moment he sees you when you return.
- He is already panting when you return home.
- There is evidence of drooling.

Excessive greeting

- Very high-energy greetings.
- Restless pacing.
- Takes a long time to calm down.

Monitoring you

- Heightened sensitivity to any hint of your leaving routine.
- Sometimes misjudges and starts to worry.
- Needs to keep a close eye on you in case you start the leaving process.

CAUGHT ON CAMERA

If you suspect that your dog is stressed when you leave him, check it out using video, web cam, security cameras, or sneak back and observe him unawares. For dogs that struggle with being left, life can be very difficult. Sometimes the anticipation can be almost as bad as your absence. If the video shows disturbing evidence, seek professional help.

WHY IS IT SO HARD FOR MY DOG?

It is so hard because you are so important to him. However, if you have become too important to him, it may not only impinge on your freedom, it may also mean that your dog spends a significant amount of his life in a stressed state. This situation is generally due to one of three circumstances:

Your dog is overly attached to you

The overly attached dog may follow you everywhere, possibly seeking to be in physical contact with you, or he may be fine as long as he knows he is able to get access to you. He will be unable to settle and relax unless these conditions are met. He will try to sleep on your lap, close beside you, or on your bed. The issue may have existed since puppyhood, or it may have developed during an illness when you and your dog spent a more intensive time together, or possibly after the dog had a fearful experience.

He has had a fearful experience in your absence

This could be a break-in, a flood or fire, fireworks, a car crashing outside the house. It could be something more regular such as the refuse collection, the windows being cleaned or thunder, or something that you were unaware of, such as an explosive noise from next door. He may simply have panicked as a puppy when first left on his own. These experiences may be sufficiently frightening to trigger separation issues, but the problem will be even more exaggerated if your dog is over-reliant on your reassurance and physical contact when he is frightened at other times.

He is also anxious as to how you will respond when you get back

This dog may have had mild or no stress initially, but because he has been told off when he expected a greeting, he is now confused and anxious. The telling off (with or without physical reprimand) may have been for toileting or destructive behaviour when he was a youngster, but a dog cannot relate his former misdeed that happened three hours, three minutes, or even three seconds earlier with your present anger. He therefore finds himself in a conflict situation – longing for you to come back home and wanting your fuss, while also dreading your return because you might be horrible or you might be nice. He has no way of predicting your response. The 'guilty look' you think you see is not because he knows he has done wrong; he is trying to avoid your threats and not provoke you any further. See Telling off/Punishing, page 76.

MINE!

As humans, we struggle with the canine concept of ownership. For a dog, ownership of an item is not to do with fairness or what your owner bought specifically for you; it's to do with possession – what the dog has in his keeping at that particular moment. There may be intrinsic value in what a dog has got hold of (the Sunday joint, for example) and you can understand why he is reluctant to give it up. But for some dogs, any item – no matter how worthless it is –

THE INNOCENCE OF THE GUILTY LOOK

How can you prove to yourself that the 'guilty look' is regarding his expectation of your behaviour rather than what he has done earlier?

Try leaving the house as if you were going out, but come back immediately and check as you would normally for toileting/destructive behaviour.

It is human logic to effusively praise and fuss your dog if he has been good in your absence, and tell him off or ignore him if he has been naughty. But because it makes no sense to the dog, it is the start of many separation anxiety problems.

becomes valuable if you show an interest and want to take it from him. In no time, this can become another minefield of miscommunication resulting in tension, stress and conflict.

FOOD STEALING

The strong, opportunistic streak in dogs has meant that both historically and present-day 'wild' or street dogs can often survive and thrive in situations where no meals are provided. Food is scavenged, stolen and hunted; the dogs that are the best opportunists are, inevitably, the best fed.

Most of our pampered pets still show this behaviour despite adequate feeding or, in some cases, overfeeding. When the opportunity to eat something presents itself, a dog will rarely turn it down. So your evening meal that was defrosting, the butter left on the table, the packet of crisps abandoned while you answered the phone, the child's hand-held biscuit – all gone – gobbled up almost before you noticed.

LOOK AT THE CLUES IN THIS SEQUENCE

The stance...he freezes avoiding eye contact.

How he holds his neck in relation to his shoulders, and in relation to his head...

Where his head and eyes are pointing...

The tension and wrinkling of his mouth and muzzle.

The owner could have backed off after seeing the initial clues (first photo) and, at another time, worked at building trust rather than practising conflict.

It is clearly unacceptable behaviour in the family home but your dog is just doing what dogs do – being a survivor, an opportunist. The 'weird' dogs are those that have never attempted to steal. How would they ever survive without a human? Those that have learnt – by human management and/or guile – that stealing doesn't work have a healthy but controlled appetite.

The importance and preoccupation over food is so much greater for dogs than it is for us, which is why it is such an effective training tool. But it can also be perceived as a source of competition. You may find that your dog opts to settle near you when he is chewing, or he may even 'ask' you to hold a chew so he can get a better purchase on it. In this situation, enjoy the trust your dog is showing in you. But for some dogs any interest shown in them, or the food item, is regarded as a challenge. He gobbles or chews faster, or does a swift head turn away from you with the item held firmly in his mouth, or he may even go still, thinking about warning you to back off.

TRIGGERING INFLATION

Your interest increases the value of any item. The more interest you show, the greater the value, and therefore the greater his need to defend it. Show no interest – walk out of the room. The dog might even drop it and follow you – that is how much your behaviour can can increase or decrease the value. What is it about our body language that is so easily misinterpreted? Once again, it is where our eyes are looking or focusing that is the major challenge. As soon as a resource-guarding dog is aware of your presence, he's checking to see where you are looking. Look at the item in question and he reads it as a potential challenge. It won't mean anything to the untrusting dog that you just wanted to see 'what he's got' or 'where he is', in dog parlance, if you continue looking at him, you are presenting a challenge. The more you are concerned about what your dog has in his mouth, the more your body language is open to misinterpretation.

This is why dogs that steal – or even swallow – potentially injurious items, such as socks, pebbles or remote controls, so often become highly stressed and even aggressive. You obviously place high value on those pebbles, that remote control, or that cat faeces because you want them, too:

- You present a challenge by looking at, or going over to your dog.
- You confirm that challenge by threatening or telling him off, and taking it further by actually removing the item from him.
- You may think he can be possessive or a resource-guarder, but he thinks you are even worse, since you will actually take the object out of his mouth – what sort of dog are you?

WHAT IS HE TRYING TO TELL ME?

What your dog does with his toys or chew items can be highly revealing in terms of his relationship with his human family. How readily he takes an item can be more an indication of greediness than possessiveness, but what about the dog that gets worried when something is clearly offered to him and backs away? He may turn away or back off with either a head movement or a whole body movement, clearly indicating that he does not trust the invitation. Even if you hadn't intended it, the dog who tries to create distance between the two of you regards you as competition or as a threat.

When your dog has some desirable item, such as a chew or a bone, what is his reaction? He may scuttle off to a distant safe 'den' or he may settle where he his, with no desire for privacy. He may be relaxed if you are around, or he may be shifty, keeping an eye on you so he knows what you are doing. If you come into a room when your dog is lying with his bone, his intensity of focus and the tension or stillness in his body, will tell you whether your presence is welcome or threatening. An increase in the speed of chewing, or fresh attempts to swallow it, tell you that your dog is worried you will intervene.

Sometimes that initial trust training that you do with your puppy, ensuring that he is happy to swap or give up an item, can be over-practised to the point where he fails to understand the exercise. The result is that he becomes increasingly anxious because he rarely gets the chance to enjoy the uninterrupted pleasure of having a whole meal, chew or bone all to himself whilst in your presence. If a dog willingly does a swap/exchange then you only need to revise it on an occasional basis. If, during this process, you encounter any early sign of aggression – stop. You have tried to move on too fast, so leave it for that day. If

you repeat it again and see tense body language – stop. Don't try again until you get professional help. Equally, the owner of a dog that growls as soon as you enter the room should also get professional help before attempting to change the dog's attitude.

"I DON'T WANT IT – BUT YOU'RE NOT HAVING IT!"

It seems ludicrous to us that a dog may try to cover up his unfinished breakfast with bedding or a mat, quite bizarre that he may go from place to place trying to bury his chew down the back of the settee or under a cushion, in the dirty washing or in the fireplace. The dog may be satiated but food items are held in such high regard, he cannot give them up. If you see these behaviours, consider not giving your dog that type of chew/bone, or try cutting his food down. He may be finding the over abundance of food stressful, but how would you know? The dog that takes a chew and buries it, perhaps after exploring a few options, and then forgets it, expends little mental energy and doesn't get wound up.

However, other dogs may spend up to two hours trying to find the right place, moving the chew/bone again and again. Once it is in situ, the dog still cannot relax, as he feels the need to keep guard. He may rush back to the hiding place if you or someone else ventures vaguely in that direction. At its most extreme, this type of dog ends up panting and wide-eyed with a responsibility that interferes with his ability to relax. He needs you to be less generous but more kind.

MY PLACE

Ownership of a toy box, a dog bed, your bed or a chair develops in two major ways: firstly, through the pattern of always going to that place; secondly, and most importantly for the dog, a build up of familiar scents, such as his saliva on toys, and hair and scent on bedding and furniture.

Move a dog's bed or 'his' chair around in a room and the dog will select 'his' bedding. Some dogs become very attached to their bedding and will try to grab it or mount it as you remove it for cleaning. At its most stressful, a dog may even stiffen or give warning barks or growls. It is as if he experiences confusion or conflict when his home base is moved.

CONVINCING THE WORRIER YOU ARE NEITHER COMPETITION, NOR THREAT

Helping Out

Give your dog a long-lasting chew

When he is chewing
Quietly throw high-value treats, e.g. cheese/chicken, towards him. Be generous.

When he takes the treats and doesn't immediately go back to the chew
Throw treats so that he has to move to get them.

When he behaves as above
Without looking towards the chew, begin to approach it, all the while throwing treats near it and away from it.

Provided he is more interested in the treats than the chew
- Hand-feed him, moving increasingly closer to the chew.
- While treating, begin to reach out to touch the chew, pick it up and immediately put it down again.
- Offer him the chew from one hand and a supply of tasty treats from the other hand.

Providing he chooses the treats
Put the treats away in your pocket and offer him the chew.

Note:
Any time he chooses the chew over the treats, let him have it (you were too slow, or too mean, when offering the treats). Be aware of your body language; no movement should suggest you are interested in the chew. While you will need to repeat some of this process, don't do it every time he has a chew.

Standing, not sitting on the sofa, with tense furrowed brow, head and tail lowered suggest this dog is expecting a challenge. Perhaps getting him off the sofa used to be his game? It certainly isn't now.

The tools that we use to manage our dogs, such as food bowls and leads, are generally kept in specific places. The dog that is keen to be fed, or to go out, soon works out that going to that place… looking at you… looking at that place… looking at you… looking at that place… often starts the feed/walk process. Many a visiting dog walker or house sitter experiences great pleasure in being shown the ropes by the resident dog!

Of course, succumbing to the dog's 'eye pointing', for instance: looking at the treat cupboard… you… treat cupboard… you… means hope on the dog's part easily becomes frustration when you ignore him, or you look and talk to him, but don't go to the cupboard.

With frustration comes escalating behaviours: perhaps a whine, a bark, or an increase in movement – perhaps moving over to you and then back to the 'place'. In the early stages of this behaviour, you will probably have responded to the increased demand, inadvertently rewarding it. Over the days and weeks or years, our varied response – mostly responding, sometimes trying to ignore it, occasionally responding – strengthens the behaviour until it spirals out of control. The dog barks, jumps up, whines and spins to elicit the 'right' response. Trying to make him stop by shouting, or by giving him commands to sit, etc., while momentarily reducing or inhibiting the excited behaviours, can, overall, lead to an increase in intensity. Faster movement, a higher pitched bark, or big avoidance behaviours may be the result. This increase in arousal is due to the element of fear that your annoyance or anger has provoked. If your dog is displaying such behaviour, understanding that it was, you, who unintentionally taught him in the first place, may help to resolve the situation.

THE GOOD OLD DAYS

You can put a stop to your dog's frustration by going back to the days when he didn't know where his treats were stored, or where you hung his lead. Change the location of where you keep the object of his desires, keep changing your pattern of behaviour, and put a stop to responding to his eye pointing and his accompanying demands. Remember how easily he trained you last time!

MY PERSON

A bitch with her newborn puppies will be very concerned about their whereabouts, and will want to be very near them. She may become agitated if a human interferes. Some adult dogs will also do this with unrelated puppies, or with a very close canine companion. We also see this with some dogs taking on a nanny role with human babies and toddlers in their family. This seems to be an instinctive behaviour and is characterised by an intense or even obsessive interest in knowing where the infant, dog or human is, and wanting to be close at hand.

However, the dog who resents another human approaching his special person is a different story. First you need to find out if it is that particular person the dog is concerned about, in which case he will show completely different body language if he is approached in an identical manner when he is on his own. If he is resource-guarding a particular person, there will be a display of tension or increased activity only when he is close to that person.

The little lap dog that grumbles or snarls as someone approaches his preferred person is nearly always told off, or even worse, taken off the lap as punishment. How much worse is it when that person approaches now – not only is that person scary but

Your dog may react aggressively when he's on your lap and someone else approaches. It doesn't necessarily mean he is guarding you, or being possessive, if he also shows concern when he is not with you.

his preferred person turns inexplicably horrible and eviction can be expected, naturally compounding the dog's desire to keep other people away.

Another interesting scenario can occur between joint owners when one owner dislikes the way the other owner interacts with the dog and communicates this by tone of voice, body tension, gesture or change in breathing. The dog, appreciating the support, becomes more confident in repelling his co-owner. This type of coalition usually develops when one owner is acutely aware of the dog's emotions and feelings and tries to protect him from his co-owner. The co-owner may be doing his best to make friends with the dog: approaching whilst talking to him, fussing and petting him, ignoring the freezing, lip licking, yawning, turning away or maybe even the grumbling or snarling. Equally, the dog is doing his best to ask him to back off. Owners are often amazed at how ignoring and taking the focus off interaction leads to the dog being happier and wanting to interact more.

EFFECTIVE IGNORING

Ignoring is a strategy for thwarting an unwanted behaviour that is often promoted by trainers, behaviourists and the dog whispering brigade. It has a surprisingly narrow area of usefulness but when it is the appropriate strategy – and done well – it is gentle and very effective.

Ignoring is only of use if the unwanted behaviour

Digging feels good to a dog so ignoring it won't stop the behaviour – unless he's hoping you will chase him!

is aimed at getting your attention, or a reaction from you. It is limited to situations where the dog is, in some way, asking. For example, if you do something for the dog when he asks, such as opening the door or getting his supper. Or it could involve you doing something to the dog, again when he asks for it, such as petting him, playing with him, giving him attention by looking at him or talking to him.

However, ignoring as a strategy is useless for clarifying behaviour if the chosen behaviour is self-rewarding or intrinsically satisfying. If the dog is doing something he wants to do (chewing/eating/chasing/playing/cleaning himself), or if it increases his arousal (sexual/physical, or excitement levels) ignoring will be of no consequence. If the dog wants to do it, an ignoring programme will have no effect However, if a behaviour is in its infancy – a puppy barking or jumping up for attention – given time, and not responding as the dog wants, can be highly effective, as long as this strategy is adopted consistently.

Consistency is important with whatever strategy you select to alter a behaviour, but with ignoring it is more than important, it is crucial. Inconsistency – sometimes ignoring, but sometimes not – makes the problem worse. It makes the unwanted behaviour stronger and more resistant to change.

You, as an individual, may have been inconsistent or there may have been inconsistency among family members but, as far as the dog is concerned, he will keep trying his attention seeking behaviour as

sometimes he does get a response. You need to know exactly what behaviour(s) your dog sees as the start of your response. You may look towards him or it may be much more subtle body language, such as a slight shifting of your weight or body in his direction, or in the direction he wants you to move. This may be completely unintended on your part, but for a whole second or two the dog thought he had you – a good enough reason for him to keep on trying!

Appeasing behaviours, typically seen as licking and rolling over, should be ignored, but you also need to create more appropriate behaviour, perhaps by moving away and then immediately responding in a casual, brief and non-intense way. Bear in mind, if you ignore an appeasing dog completely, you will increase his insecurity, leading to more intense behaviours as he desperately seeks approval or acknowledgement. Create space and nurture more confident interaction.

IMPULSE CONTROL

Frustration escalates when the dog's expectation of getting what he wants is thwarted, despite continuous trying. Some dogs find it very hard when they can't get what they want/expect, and it leads to the dog losing self-control. He might resort to behaviours, such as barking at, or biting at someone/something nearby as he redirects his energy. In this situation, the dog is struggling to process what is going on around him – he is thinking only of what it is he wants. A popularly advocated technique is to ignore until the behaviour has stopped. You, therefore wait until the dog has ceased:

- Barking before you put his lead on.
- Spinning before you put his meal down.
- Yipping before you open the door.
- Madly scratching at you before you play with him.

This strategy may work with a dog that isn't easily frustrated, but it is a completely illogical approach for a dog struggling with self-control. It serves only to increase the frustration and, with that, the dog's arousal and stress levels. This renders the dog even less capable of making any sense of what you are doing. The longer you stick it out, the more frustrated, and the less compos mentis, the dog will be. It is so much easier to resolve frustration problems by reducing the frustration.

What a clear picture the owner of this mouthing Staffie is giving. For frustrated dogs this strategy is more likely to be successful in an interesting environment where that energy will be redirected into exploring.

PRE-EMPTING FRUSTRATION

Set up a situation so that your dog, initially, experiences zero frustration. Let him have what he wants before he shows any unwanted behaviour – before he even thinks about it.

After a number of repetitions, when he is no longer expecting to be frustrated, he will be much calmer and will be in a mental state where he can learn a new behaviour.

Very gradually, extend the time he waits for what he wants. Whether he is waiting for just a second and remaining calm, or briefly assumes a sit, for example, reward it profusely.

Tip: In a new situation, or with a puppy, do this from the beginning. Whatever he wants will be the reward – there is no need to use treats.

TELLING OFF/PUNISHING

In the old school of dog training, physical punishment was considered a legitimate means of training, and the first choice to stop unwanted behaviour. Nowadays, this is not only considered cruel and inhumane, but its effect – based on fear and avoidance – is not appropriate for learning new, more appropriate behaviours. Obviously there are occasions when you need to intervene and dramatically interrupt an undesirable behaviour – such as when your dog is about to steal food from a worktop – but also when his safety is jeopardised – if he is trying to leap out of the car window, for example.

What is the most effective method to use? In a dog's eyes, telling off/punishment can look very different from how we intend it. Reprimands can be obvious and very undesirable, such as rolling the dog over/pinning or holding him down, lead jerks, hitting or tapping him. Or they can be more subtle, but still highly significant as far as the dog is concerned. These include verbal warnings (bah! no! ahah! sssh!) or using his name in a harsh tone, eye-balling, eye-balling with your head and shoulders lowered towards him, approaching in a threatening manner, or finger wagging/pointing.

Telling off or punishment should not be used for any situation where the behaviour might have an emotional basis:

* Fear/distress, e.g. barking when left alone.
* Frustration, e.g. pulling on the lead towards a friend.
* Aggressive displays to other dogs or people.
* Relationship miscommunications, e.g. jumping up during greeting or puppy play biting.

Any behaviourist will tell you that a high proportion of such behavioural problems are actually caused, distorted, or made worse by telling off or punishment. Isolated behaviours, or those involving inanimate objects carry less potential fall-out. For example:

* Jumping up to the kitchen worktop.
* Eating cat faeces.
* Barging past or crashing into you when playing.

When managed effectively, these behaviours can be quickly stopped. But, in order to be fair, the following criteria must be adhered to:

* The person applies it with perfect timing just as the dog is about to, or has started, the unwanted behaviour – not a second later or earlier.
* The person is 100 per cent sure of what the dog is thinking about doing at the second of application so there is no doubt as to what he will associate with the threat/pain/startle.

- The type and degree of punishment has been selected at exactly the right level for that particular dog, at that particular time, and for that particular behaviour. It is sufficient to stop the behaviour without causing anything other than momentary startle/pain/stress.
- The dog already knows and can choose an alternative, acceptable behaviour.

If all the above is in place, repeating two or three times in a given situation quickly reduces the punishment needed to an occasional (if ever) subtle warning.

From this, it can be seen that telling off/punishment is extremely hard to do well – in fact, almost impossible – which is why it should be avoided. The fall-out from not doing it perfectly can be horrendous for the dog and lead to a breakdown of the dog/owner relationship.

MISLEADING DRAMA

Telling off might lead to the cessation of the unwanted behaviour, but might have serious, detrimental side effects. The most obvious example is the big media dog trainer who wants instant 'miraculous' results – but at what cost? The following questions should be asked:

1. Why has the behaviour ceased?
2. What does the dog think of the person applying the punishment?
3. What does the dog think about his 'misbehaviour?'

Look at the dog's body language to inform your understanding. You may well find that the result is often gained when the dog is physically exhausted so has less energy to resist. Or it could be that the dog is forced into the situation and so must give up or continue to be threatened/hurt. There is no other choice. He shuts down.

There is fear – a great deal of fear – it is not 'respect' or being 'lower in the pack'. It is just fear, pure and simple. If you look carefully, you will see the dog trying to get away and using avoidance techniques such as lip licking and looking away. Look at the tension in his face and his lips and the prolonged panting. No, he certainly doesn't want to do the behaviour in question, he doesn't even want to be there, and certainly doesn't

Appeasement to concern to defence

Having a history of being corrected for getting up on the sofa, this sweet dog is very suspicious of her owner's invitation..

Appeasingly she drops her shoulders and lowers her neck before getting up.

When there, she desperately pushes her head into her owner. The tension shown through her body, and in her facial features, is dramatic.

She worries about being challenged, and although it wasn't intended, she perceives the owner as doing just that and, therefore, acts in self-defence.

want to be with that trainer – who is just about to advocate that the owner now replicates his methods...

Don't be fooled by the 'calmness' of the dog. It has just shut down/opted out/given up because there was no choice. Don't be fooled by: "see, he still wants to be with me", or "he's fine now" as the dog is desperately giggly and playful as huge relief kicks in as he realises that the ordeal is now over. Don't be fooled by: "see, he still loves me" as the dog does his repertoire of appeasing/approval-seeking behaviours, such as jumping up, leaning against, nudging, licking, or even trying to get to the trainer's mouth. Anything that will elicit something other than another telling off – anything that will make him feel less threatened.

HOME TRUTHS ABOUT TELLING OFF

There are three elements to bear in mind:

1. TIMING

So often the timing isn't right so your dog has no way of connecting his action with your reaction:

Too late:
If you find yourself saying: "look what you've done", you are probably too late. The dog has finished the misdemeanour before you have even opened your mouth. If you are shutting him in the crate or kitchen because of something he did in the sitting room – you are too late. If you are being rough with him, or not talking to him because of something he did on the walk earlier – forget it, he has no idea what you are on about. If you are continuing to tell him off even though he has stopped doing the unwanted behaviour, you are making no sense.

Too early:
If you are threatening him as you leave the house because of past destruction or barking – back off! That's not fair – what if he was going to do the right thing, this time?

You need to be sure your dog will make the right connections so, therefore, you need to know what his present focus and understanding is.

The lowered ears, neck and back, and eyes looking upwards, are signs of fear – not guilt.

2. THE WRONG SUBJECT

Surprise or startle based reprimands, such as lead checks, spray collars, hitting/tapping, and rattle can lead to devastating consequences if used on behaviours involving other people or other dogs. If the other dog, or person, is using normal, unthreatening body language, the dog will quickly learn to mistrust such communication. Being startled in such ways leads many a dog to disbelieving the innocent body language of their own species – how dare we!

3. CONSISTENCY

When a dog is given a telling off by one person for getting on the settee, but someone else lets it go, how should he behave? When one minute you throw the toy for him every time he drops it in your lap, and the next you shout at him because you have had enough, or you are watching a good film, it just doesn't make sense.

It is very hard, to be clear and consistent, but it is essential if you choose to correct or tell off.

THE NEED TO RECONSIDER

Most of us have come across a dog that flinches when you lift your arm to scratch your head, or suddenly ducks as your hand approaches his head/face. There is many a dog who skulks off to hide when he hears raised voices.

The telling off may or may not have resulted in the dog learning to stop the behaviour, but now he no longer trusts the everyday movements or tones of voice of the human race.

This may not have been the legacy intended but it is often the outcome. Conversely, there are dogs who have gradually become desensitised to threats by shouting and gesture. The owner may have started out gently and, over time, has had to keep going up a level to get an effect, and now has to physically intervene.

When you use punishment and telling off as the main way to change your dog's behaviour, you need to be constantly on the look out for misdemeanours,

and always ready to respond. This negative approach is tiring and stressful for both of you and, thankfully, never necessary.

HELPING HIM MAKE THE RIGHT CHOICE

It isn't necessary or helpful in the long-term to reprimand your dog. Understanding why he might do the unwanted behaviour will enable you to create a situation where it won't happen. Knowing him well enough to predict his weaknesses means you can:

Manage: Avoid or minimise the temptation.
Pre-empt: Before he does it, re-direct him elsewhere or to another behaviour.
Associate: Make the behaviour you would prefer he did highly rewarding.

SUMMING UP

Routines and patterns are easily learnt by our dogs. This can be relaxing or lead to the earlier and earlier anticipation of an event. This relates specifically to the dog who is anxious about being left alone. In fact, no dog would choose to be left at home alone – most learn to tolerate it. There are many indicators that let you know how easy/hard it is for each, particular dog.

Taking an item away from a dog, looking at, or approaching him, will increase the value he ascribes to that item. Dogs are happy to share if you build up trust. Unwanted behaviours that are based on frustration are more quickly, and more easily, changed by pre-empting rather than ignoring or waiting for the dog to 'give up'. Telling off a frustrated dog can lead to displays of aggressive or appeasement behaviours. Your job is to manage temptations; pre-empt them and redirect your dog to alternative, rewarding behaviours.

Telling off/correction is hard to do clearly and kindly. It is based on creating a fear response. It is often detrimental to the dog's trust in the perpetrator – and to other people. Punishment/dominance/leadership challenges are undesirable and unnecessary for a calm, relaxed household.

Chapter Seven

WHAT ARE YOU ASKING FOR?

Opening up channels of communication in training

A dog doesn't arrive in your home knowing what you expect from him – in fact, he has no idea what you consider to be desirable or undesirable behaviour.

However, he has some ideas of his own – and those are to do with his innate dogginess, prompting him to follow his own instincts and desires. For everyone's safety, social acceptance and physical comfort, dogs need to receive training in lead walking, recall and some degree of stay/wait.

When you train your dog you are working on two fronts:

• Encouraging and rewarding the behaviour you want so your dog will repeat it and it will become part of his established repertoire.

• Discouraging the behaviour you don't want by ignoring it, modifying it, or fast tracking past it so your dog's desire to repeat it lessens and eventually disappears.

Sounds simple? Well, the principles are, but the business of communicating what we want frequently comes unstuck, leaving the dog feeling confused and anxious, or even aggressive, as he fails to understand our meaning. However, it doesn't have to be this way if we open our minds – and our eyes – so we can find out what is going on. Every dog gives off clear signals which will tell you if he understands what you want and if he is motivated to do it. He will also show you when he is muddled, disinterested, or worried by the task he has been set. Your job is to pick up on the clues and adjust your training programme to suit his individual needs and his own unique personality.

A BLANK SLATE

Think about something you are good at; a particular skill you have acquired, such as driving a car or baking a cake. Now try to remember your first efforts when you had no knowledge or experience to draw on. Over time, and with continued exposure to your chosen craft, you have refined your skills and became the expert that you are today. What you now find easy, and scarcely need to think about, required guidance in the early days of learning. Expertise is not something you were born with; it is something that has to be nurtured, and fine-tuned over a period of time. If you want your dog to become expert at something, whether it is as simple as learning to sit when you ask him, or as complex as teaching him to come back to you regardless of what he has to leave, he needs you to take him through the process, step-by-step.

The best trainers excel at this. Not only are they good at breaking down tasks into small steps, but they also use their knowledge and experience to decide which step to start on and how to progress. By erring on the side of caution, they ensure the dog or person in their hands is always successful.

EXPLAINING WITHOUT WORDS

Dogs understand little, or nothing, of spoken language; neither are they very good at imitating us. We are, therefore, relatively limited in how we can explain a new skill we want them to learn. In reward-based training there are three methods of trying to elicit a behaviour:

Luring: Letting the dog follow a treat, or reward, to the position, or place, of your choosing.

Guiding: Using your body, or structures in the environment, to create opportunities that allow the dog to access his reward by choosing the desired position, or place.

Shaping: Accepting and rewarding an offered behaviour from the dog which will increasingly approximate the end behaviour.

When you are training, ideally, you should have the flexibility to dance between these methods, depending on what it is you wish to teach, and how your dog best learns in a particular situation. You need to work out how to achieve the end behaviour and find out what method you, and your dog, are most skilled and comfortable with. As with all training clarity is key.

CLEAR COMMUNICATION

MAKING IT WORTH DOING AGAIN
Very few dogs will be keen to stay engaged with you, and work to learn new behaviours, simply for praise or petting. In fact, if you watch your dog's body language when you are praising and petting him for a 'good' behaviour, you are likely to observe him ducking his head, or moving away from such attention – he's hardly going to risk that again!

Your choice of treat/toy will also affect his level of commitment – both his concentration and how hard he will try. Turn on his senses with smelly, easy-to-swallow treats or squeaky, fluffy toys – whatever he likes best! The value can be increased further by making the reward chaseable.

YOU ARE MAGIC!
We want our dogs to do the behaviour even if we haven't got a treat/toy on show. As soon as possible, make sure the reward is out of sight, but magically

WHY IS HE GETTING IT WRONG?

A dog, like a human toddler, never intentionally gets it wrong – unless you have let him find it rewarding (interesting/exciting).

He isn't wrong if:
- You haven't found a way to explain the exercise to him in a way he understands.
- You are not motivating him enough to want to do it.
- You haven't prepared him for this situation.
- He's not sure what you are asking because:
  - you are saying things differently
  - you are signalling differently
  - you are behaving differently
  - you haven't helped him learn how to do the exercise in this environment.

MAKING IT EASY

- Remember, like you, your dog is not a computer. It will take quite a few successful attempts on a few occasions before he truly 'gets it'.
- When training a new behaviour, keep as many of the external factors in each session as similar as possible, e.g. same place, same orientation, same treats. Generalisation (taking the learnt behaviour to different places) and proofing (challenging it) are for later.
- By allowing yourself only 10-20 treats to use as rewards in one session, you can give yourself thinking time to assess what your dog is understanding and how you can give him more help. However, make sure you have more treats on hand in case he is on the cusp of a breakthrough.

A dropped or slightly tucked tail occurs when some dogs are concentrating, but this tail is quite tightly tucked, and combined with the backward pointing ears tell us he is worried. In this instance, the trainer is luring, encouraging the dog to pick up his other front paw – but he isn't helping the dog understand. The dog tries his hardest to do what he knows – lifting his other paw as high as he can.

appears when you click or mark the behaviour (see below). Start this when your dog is reliably showing signs of understanding what is wanted.

A SALIENT CLICK OR MARKER WORD

It will be easier for your dog to learn a range of behaviours if he only has to listen, and not look at you, to know he's right. Using a clicker, or a clicker word, to mark the exact behaviour you want, at the exact moment it is being performed, is the ideal solution. Remember that your click, or clicker word, needs to come before you move your hand to access a treat. Otherwise, the dog will focus on your hand movement, not the 'click' or your intended verbal marker.

TIMING, TIMING, TIMING

Yes, timing is everything in training – it is the most powerful tool you have to clarify what you want. Mark (with a click or a clicker word) the behaviour you are looking for during its occurrence – afterwards is too late! Click while the dog is on the agility contact, or while he is holding the dumbbell, if that is the behaviour you are training.

SUCCESS LEADS TO SUCCESS

As you revise and practise your new behaviour in other situations, observe your dog to gauge how he is feeling. Is he showing the same body language as he would in the kitchen at home, or at your regular training venue? Or is he a little slower to respond, or showing a more reserved version of the behaviour?

For the dog, being out and about is nothing like the kitchen – and you aren't behaving as you do at home either! Help him get up to speed; go back a few stages and he will soon be working as confidently as at home or in class. If your expectations allow for helping and supporting him in different and increasingly challenging situations, you won't see his work deteriorate or witness any of the behaviours that indicate he is worried or stressed. See Hint, hint, page 81.

A NO BRAINER

A stressed dog, or one who is over-excited, will not be processing information as normal. Address this issue first whether it is a five-minute, or a year-long project. Be prepared to alter your expectations if your dog starts to show evidence of negative or positive stress. Battling onwards will lead to frustration on your part, and a dog that either 'switches off' or makes unwise decisions or responses. Your dog needs you to be sensitive and use your grey matter to help him.

FRUSTRATION

Just like people, dogs have different levels and abilities at coping with frustration. While some of this is down to an individual dog's previous training experiences, some breeds or individuals are much more likely to switch off or give up sooner than others. Some breeds are also much more inclined to resort to barking behaviours if they feel frustrated. There is a degree of frustration that leads to the individual trying harder or trying new behaviours, which is very useful. But it can be that the feeling of frustration becomes too much, at

For both of these dogs the desire is very high, their body language tells us how they have been taught to wait. The Border Collie (first photo) has learnt that what he wants will be taken away if he moves before being released. With head and tail up, and ears forward, she is showing confident anticipation. In contrast, the Miniature Schnauzer (second photo) has been corrected if he moves before being released. His head is turned away, his ears are not fully forward, his facial features are tense with a disjointed eye gaze, telling us that he feels wary about what will happen next.

this particular time, for this particular dog. You need to ask yourself:

- Is he able to work calmly with 100 per cent commitment or are there some behavioural indications that he is frustrated?
- What displacement behaviours or calming signals, would he employ if it was too much for him?
- Do I know the level at which his frustration is a hindrance to his learning rather than a help?

Training can be, and should be, a bonding experience which is much enjoyed by both parties. If either you or your dog are not enjoying it – stop! Have a break, and then find a sensitive trainer who can help you, or forget it and enjoy your dog for who he is – he'll love you for it!

SHOWING, COMPETING AND TRIALLING

Competing with a dog is not for everyone, but for those who become involved in one of the canine sports, it can become an all-absorbing passion. In a best-case scenario you are spending quality time with your dog, preparing and training him, and then competing with him, which is stimulating and enjoyable for you both. But what happens when the dog's performance does not match your expectations?

Disappointment and frustration on your part can quickly lead to anxiety and stress for the dog. There is an additional concern of allowing a dog to become so over-aroused with the excitement of the sport – particularly true of agility and flyball – that it is impacting on his health and well being. Admittedly, we all like to win but if you compete with your dog, your prime concern must be to monitor his feelings and react accordingly.

A dog will be quick to pick up on your enthusiasm excitement and nervousness when you are competing; he will know if you are particularly pleased with him or whether you are upset or even angry. He is aware of all these changing emotions but he has no context for them. He has no idea that he has qualified for Crufts or that he is now a Champion.

The competition that you are involved in is a human competition, based on human values; it has no meaning or significance for your dog. So what must he be thinking when sometimes you praise him to

HINT, HINT

Helping Out

The dog that shows any of the following behaviours is trying to tell you something:

- Looking at you or getting easily distracted.
- Yawning, scratching, licking his lips, or lifting a paw.
- Play-bowing, rolling around.
- Jumping up, humping or mouthing you.
- Doing a repetitive behaviour, e.g. spinning, fly catching, tail chasing, circling.
- Going for a mad dash.
- Sniffing, marking, urinating.
- Barking at you.

If these behaviours only occur when you are training/ working your dog – he's shouting out that there is something he's not comfortable with.

the skies, maybe even hugging him (which he might obligingly tolerate!), but another time you shrug your shoulders and ignore him, or walk away in a deflated manner – all of which he will find punishing?

If you think you are communicating to your dog that you are displeased with an earlier aspect of his performance, you are mistaken. We know that punishment must be administered within the same second to make sense to the dog regardless of whether it is an active correction, such as lead jerk or a passive correction, such as ignoring him.

With his upright stance, the front dog shows high arousal and focused anticipation. The dog behind him is also highly, aroused, but he is showing frustration because he is being held back. Note the difference in ear and neck positioning, and the balance of the body weight.

Active attempts to punish him by roughly attaching the lead or route marching him away will certainly elicit a response in the form of avoidance behaviours or energised appeasing behaviours. However, the body language is not that of guilt or an understanding that he should have done better, his capacity is not that advanced. It is simply fear of your reaction.

So if your dog goes wrong halfway through a round/exercise, but finished well, your negative reaction will be interpreted as applying to the last thing he did. Badly timed and therefore totally unjustifiable correction is one of the reasons why so many performance dogs begin to show behaviours that demonstrate their confusion.

These may include:

- Not showing the same level of keenness when competing.
- Looking away or backing away from you, particularly at the start when there is a pause in the proceedings.
- Can't do his sit/wait.
- Ducks under or knocks jumps.
- Hesitating when asked to perform some, or a part of the test.

- Frustration behaviours such as barking, spinning, mouthing or grabbing.
- Wants to leave the ring/venue.

Not knowing how someone is going to respond to you – whether you are a dog or a human – and not knowing what you are being punished for or the reason you are being ignored, is both unnerving and off-putting. Even if you were able to punish your dog with appropriate timing, either in training or in competition, why are you doing it? Your dog will never intentionally get it wrong. Your preparation may be at fault; you may be unclear as to what you are asking for, you may have failed to motivate him – but these are your responsibilities, not his.

When you celebrate your dog's performance, make sure he is enjoying it as much as you! In your enthusiasm you may overlook blatant signs, such as the dog turning his head away, lowering or even ducking his head downwards, taking a little step back or doing a shake off when you finish your celebration. Some dogs will show more subtle clues – a tense mouth, lip licking, holding the ears down, averting eyes and yawning – clearly indicating their discomfort.

Dogs that are expecting to be roughed up as part

of this intended praise and reward will display their disquiet by bouncing around or mouthing. If you look closely at the body language, you may well see signs of appeasement lowering the neck, head down but eyes upwards looking at you, a wriggly rear end and a low wagging tail. All these behaviours, especially if delivered at high speed, indicate worry and concern.

OVER-AROUSAL

In order to do well in canine competition, both you and your dog must be on top form. Whether your competition requires speed, quick response or accuracy, your dog must be sufficiently aroused to have the motivation/drive or attitude to perform successfully. However, a balance has to be achieved; the fulcrum is easily tipped in the direction of over-arousal. As arousal increases, so too does the potential for negative consequences. A dog who is hyped up may:

- Over-react to other dogs or people.
- Become over-sensitive to potentially worrying things in the environment.
- Redirect his energy into barking or biting at someone or something.

HAVING AN END ROUTINE

For dogs that are sensitive to disappointment, and for handlers who are not very good at hiding it, having an end routine can help you both. For example:

- Using a tug toy, tug, pulling while you pivot around twice.
- Attach the lead and take the toy.
- Ask for a wait, and the release to grab the toy. Repeat.
- Put the toy away and throw down four treats – one after another – as you walk away.

- Lose the ability to recover quickly from a difficult experience.

These are serious consequences that soon generalise into daily life. They are the results of the dog's emotions spiralling out of control to the extent that he is no longer able to process what is happening. It is our choice to put our dogs in these situations; we owe it to them to ensure this is not the outcome.

The rear, racing dog looks alert but concerned, with tight facial features. The dog being held is all over the place both mentally and physically. He may turn out to be fast but his extreme arousal means he will struggle to process directions, and is likely to make bad decisions. His racing partner lip licks, blinks and has ears pinned back, looking very uneasy. It doesn't look as if this team are going to pull together!

84

LONG-TERM OVER-AROUSAL

Has your dog developed:

Reaction to the environment
A need to:
• Bark.
• Chew.
• Spin.
• Run.
• Engage in repetitive behaviours.

Reaction to you
• Easily frustrated.
• Easily distracted.
• Difficulty concentrating.
• Often unaware of you.
• Showing attention seeking behaviours.

Energy levels
• High!
• Adrenaline junkie – always wants more.
• Disruptions in toileting behaviour.
• In a state of constant anticipation.

Substitutes badly
• Uses non-toys as play items.
• Creates own undesirable games.
• Persists in play invites even when dog/human indicates it is unwanted.

Rest and sleep patterns
• Restless, always on the go.
• Sleeping too much/not enough.
• Difficulty settling.
• Some degree of pacing.

COMPETITION DAY

This can be a long and exhausting day for dogs and owners alike but it will be viewed from two very different perspectives. In the majority of canine sports the dog is competing for less than five minutes; in the case of agility or flyball it will be over in less than a minute. Even if the dog is entered in a number of classes and is working for half an hour each time, this still means that he is only competing for 15 per cent of the day, (based on getting ready to go to the competition at 7 am, and arriving home at 5 pm).

For the agility dog who is under the judge for a total of three minutes of the day, the percentage of time he is actually competing is 0.2 per cent – a tiny amount of his ten-hour day. So what is going on the rest of the time? It is highly likely that what happens when a dog is not competing is far more significant than the time he spends in the ring.

Even if you are confident that your dog loves the time when he is competing, you need to be brave enough to look at his emotional experiences throughout the rest of the day. There are so many aspects to the competition day that can be a source of stress, concern or over-excitement for your dog, which can have a greater impact than the small percentage of the time when he is actively taking part. You would consider yourself a neglectful owner if you did not look after your dog's physical needs on a competition day – providing him with food, water, the chance to toilet, etc. But what about his emotional needs? These are important as not only will it affect his performance but, even worse, any stress and anxiety could have long-term implications on his future well-being.

LET'S BE HONEST

If competing with your dog, you need to be honest enough to acknowledge that you are competing for your own satisfaction. It is you, not your dog, who chooses to do this. It is only by observing your dog throughout the competition day, picking up on his signalling and body language, that you will gain knowledge of his true emotional state. This will enable you to decide if you need to take any action, which could be as follows:

• Don't change anything: The dog is working at optimum level and can chill when not working.

- Provide more rest times.
- Provide better quality rest times.
- Avoid high arousal triggers.
- Allocate more time for relaxed sniffing and investigation.
- Make time to warm up, both emotionally and physically, so he is switched on to you.
- Work out an emotional and physical cool down strategy.

Do everything you can to make sure that the competition day is at least as pleasurable, if not more pleasurable, than being at home with you? Competing may be a great source of pleasure for you: enjoy it, do your very best – but don't do it at a cost to your dog.

SUMMING UP

Training is not about what you teach but about what is being learnt. We can't verbally explain to our dogs what we want so it is vital to:

- Break down the behaviour into small steps.
- Progress at the dog's rate of understanding.
- Explain using luring, guiding or shaping.
- Use a clicker or clicker word to mark the exact moment the dog performs the desired task to clarify your explanation.
- Select appropriate rewards, and consider how best to use them.

If you watch your dog's body language he will show you if he:

- Is frustrated.
- Doesn't understand.
- Doesn't feel motivated.
- Is over-aroused.
- Is worried or nervous in that environment.
- Is fearful of your response.

Competitions have been contrived by, and for, humans. We need to, consciously, keep the emotional welfare of our dogs at the top of our agenda.

IS IT ALL TOO MUCH?

Intently focusing on another competing agility dog, every muscle is tense as he prepares for a 'herding' opportunity. Although quite still, his body and brain are in a high state of arousal.

Tipping over the threshold, he will be oblivious to the jerk created as he almost pulls his owner over.

This Collie finds some relief by holding a toy in his mouth, but this level of arousal is tiring.

Chapter Eight

MEETING AND GREETING

Interactions with unfamiliar dogs

What is your definition of a sociable dog? We all have varying expectations, but most owners would agree that the perfect dog is the one you can take anywhere, who will settle quietly in a café or on the beach, ignoring all the other pestering dogs. We can let him off-lead anywhere – he never goes too far away to meet another dog, and when we move on and call him away he comes immediately. The perfect dog loves all other dogs. He never tells puppies off even when they bite and pull at him; adult dogs can also do what they want to him – he just turns the other cheek. He can give confidence to a scared dog, he can placate an aggressive dog, and the icing on the cake is that he loves to play with other canines. He will play with anyone – big or small, fast or slow – he just loves to play.

There are some dogs who fit all the above criteria and, of these, there are some who are confident and relaxed in all these scenarios. For many dogs, however, it will be easy to observe signs of tension. For others, these situations will be unbearable and lead to an aggressive display – or worse. Interestingly, there are possibly more clever canines who adopt a survival strategy that looks like play or acceptance. But, on closer observation, we can see clues that the dog would prefer to exit the interaction, or shows signs of being highly relieved when it is all over.

INHERITED OR LEARNT BEHAVIOUR?

"Is this just him, or did he learn it?" This question is often asked by those who own dogs that have problems interacting with other dogs, but it is relevant for all dog owners.

Why does your dog behave the way he does?

Fundamental to our perspective on how dogs communicate with each other is the knowledge that it takes two dogs to communicate, and this communication is highly dependent on the other dog's response. Your dog might play with one dog, exchange brief greetings with another and almost have a fight with a third dog. In different situations your dog may say and feel different things. On-lead or off-lead can be very different; at a training class he may be better or worse than he is in the park.

How much your dog wants to communicate with others, and what he says and feels, will change throughout his life. As a pup he might have been keen to lick at all dogs, as a teenager he might have been desperate to play, as an adult he may be keen to greet and might play, and in his old age he may show little interest in other dogs. Taking this understanding as a starting point, let us now examine 10 different types of interactions (categories) and find out when you should intervene either for your dog's sake, or to help the other dog.

1. "PLEASE BE MY FRIEND"

This is a greeting of friendly intention, typified by a wagging tail and undulating body, a dipped back, shoulders and neck lowered as he heads towards the other dog – maybe licking near the mouth as he gets closer. There is nothing to suggest a threat or a warning; the dog is showing appeasing behaviour, sometimes flicking his tongue out of the mouth towards the other dog, in the hope that the other dog will view him kindly and will not be aggressive. This appeasing licking is seen in all puppies to some degree, and in some interactions with adult dogs, but for the naturally appeasing dog this display is deeply ingrained and persists through adulthood. There is clearly a genetic element as some breeds and some lines are much more likely to use appeasing behaviours than others.

Looking into space, the adult tolerantly turns his head away. The appeasing youngster, with ears pinned back, cautiously stretches forward to sniff.

THE EXTREME VERSION: "Please, please, please be my friend"

When this dog is told off or rebuffed, he doesn't walk away; his appeasing behaviours become more exaggerated. He desperately tries to lick around the other dog's mouth, his shoulders are further lowered – even to the ground – and his head is held up, almost vertical. His rump is almost on the ground, possibly with hind legs spreading, and his tail is held low but

wagging, probably clamped between his legs. The likelihood of this dog rolling over on to his back and going into a freeze is high, especially for pups. The response of the other dog determines whether the squirming increases or abates.

If he receives a very frightening telling off, he will back off or freeze and will not pursue the issue. If, however, the telling off was frightening but perceived as a warning only – with no intention of aggression – he will momentarily back off and then his appeasing behaviours will be intensified. The 'nicer' the other dog, the worse it is. Dogs that are ineffective at telling the appeasing dog to go away can be tormented by this extremist; the more half-hearted the tell-off, the more the extremist is determined to try and gain his approval. If the appeasing dog is nervous as well as needy he will, initially, use appeasing behaviour but as soon as the other dog turns or moves away, he will dart in with a defensive warning which could take the form of barking, air snaps or a partial lunge.

HELP OUT!

If this is your dog, help out and separate the dogs. Call your dog away for a treat after only a brief greeting has been exchanged. What a relief this will be for all concerned! Watch out for the shake off, the yippy bounce or short dash – all clearly saying: "Phew! I don't have to carry on with this nonsense!"

2. "SHALL WE PLAY?"

Some dogs, especially dogs under two or three years old, may be very hopeful and approach all dogs with a play questioning body. The more experienced dog

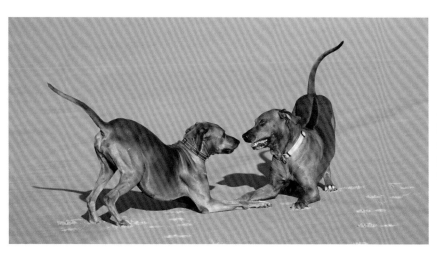

A delightful example of mirroring. The soft, open mouths and the overlapping front legs are clues to their ease with each other.

may start his play invites quite subtly, with the display getting faster and bolder if he is not rebuffed. These invitations involve little bursts of sudden movements which may involve contact – brief nose or paw nudges for a second or so – or it may be in gesture form, without any contact. The well-known play bow, where elbows are flung on the ground while the rear end remains in the air, has two subtler forms. There is a two-paw slam; this might be a high impact slam but the elbows hardly drop – it is the head and neck that bounce, but the rest of the body doesn't. The other type of play bow involves a bouncing turn around, where one dog offers himself to be chased.

Depending on the breed and/or past play experiences, different styles will be adopted. For some, running as fast as possible (for as long as possible) will be the main element of play, for others being up on their hind legs and boxing will be predominant. For others, pretend grabs at hind legs, body and neck grabs will be the main feature. Difference in size matters not nearly as much as differences in style, but the ability to read each other – and moderate their play style – determines whether play develops or one dog gives up.

THE EXTREME VERSION: "I know you really want to!"

The extremist is the dog that forces the pace – "you will play with me" or "I know you really want to" – are the demands being made. The extremist not only keeps on and on with his invitations, regardless of attempted brush-offs, he also gets rougher and louder. He pays less attention to the other dog's eyes and face – more happens from the side and behind as play becomes more and more one-sided.

Watch the interactions closely: the other dog may be feeling really uncomfortable or even unsafe as he tries to end the game. His play is half-hearted and short in duration, interspersed with attempts at walking away/sniffing/ looking at or going to his owner before returning for a short play in an attempt to keep the extremist at bay. Having tried to say "no" politely, without intervention, his 'victim' is left with three options:

- Play – even though he doesn't want to.
- Shut down – freeze, be totally non-reactive so the other dog gets bored and goes away.

- Shout louder – work up through polite warning (lifting lips, snarling, air snapping) to aggressive display (barking, lunging), escalating to aggression (making fleeting contact, or mock fight display).

He is obviously having fun trying to push the other dog – sometimes getting a bit more play and sometimes being told off, which can be exciting and almost addictive. But he is perfecting his ability to ignore polite requests, and even warnings, which could have dire consequences when interacting with dogs who are not prepared to back down.

Over time, the play enforcer becomes the victim of his own practices as he, increasingly, uses aggression to pre-empt the rebuffs and aggressive displays that he pushed others into. The dog who "always wanted to play with everyone" becomes the aggressor.

The Retriever lies on his back posing no threat but, with drawn lips, warns the other dog. The German Shepherd type isn't pushing his weight closer.

Although still engaging in play, the Border Collie bares all his teeth. He would really appreciate his owner creating a break as his playmate isn't heeding his request. Both are lightly hackled.

One solution is to keep the play-enforcer on-lead, preferably on a long lead, and work on a really positive association for coming away. This means that when the other dog starts to say "no" you can limit interactions, blocking any fun he might get from further pestering. Moving him slightly out of the way will give the other dog a chance to restart play if he chooses to. It doesn't take long before the play enforcer works out that the other dog will only come and ask for more play when he is polite.

Bear in mind, if you are not sure if your dog is enjoying the play – he isn't. You have noticed his "I'm not comfortable" clues – so help him...

3. "YOU SMELL SO INTERESTING..."
Meeting a new dog often involves sniffing each other's mouths, rears and genitals, circling and swapping around for up to 10 seconds, and then moving off or initiating play. This scenario often, but not exclusively, involves a young male who may or may not, be entire. His behaviour will be intense, maybe licking urogenital areas or just tasting the immediate air space. Ears, mouth and between shoulders will also be investigated. He would like to spend much longer than a polite 10 seconds, but when the other dog says "that's enough!" or "shall we play?" he concedes.

Not wanting to be investigated, the Labrador sits on the source of interest! Her mouth is tense as she turns to keep an eye on the inquisitive Dalmatian. She would appreciate help if he persists.

THE EXTREME VERSION: "Oh! I forgot – you are a dog"
This is almost exclusively the domain of the entire male, and especially the adolescent entire male. He is hardly interested in the front end – it's all about getting every minute detail about this dog from urogenital information. His sniffing is so urgent that he might force the other dog to lift a hind leg. He stays focused on the back end to such an extent that he becomes unaware of anything the other dog – male or female – might be trying to tell him. The other dog may tolerate this behaviour for a few seconds, but he is often forced into bouncing away, tail tucked tightly under, sitting or lying down, barking, freezing, air snapping or lunging. It often takes a significant display of aggression to get this extremist to back off.

Or your dog will soon expect all dogs to show aggression, and he will then decide to be the initiator.

AVOIDING PROBLEMS
If you are lucky, your dog will be relaxed and easy-going and have no problems with meeting other dogs. However, it will certainly help if you make meetings as stress-free as possible, which can be achieved with a little care and forward planning. If you are introducing a new dog or puppy to your household or friendship group, it is especially important to work through the hints and tips (below) to ensure long-term success.

Distraction attraction
Meet in an environment that is new to both dogs.
Think... smells that might interest them.

It's as if I knew you already
Try to organise it so that each dog gets the chance to spy on the other.
Think... scent, sight – and then take turns at following behind.

Short and sweet
Keep initial contacts brief and be quiet and calm when it is time to separate.
Think... sharing a ground scent is an easy start.
Think... move away first so your dog finds it easy to end the interaction and follow you.

Little and often
Several short and sweet meetings on several occasions will see you well on your way.
Think... when your dog tells you:" this is boring", you have succeeded!

4. "I WOULD JUST LIKE TO GET MY LEG OVER"

This behaviour is not restricted to entire males or even castrated males; females, spayed or not, may behave in a similar way. Perhaps this is the clue that enables us to understand that it isn't purely about procreation. The interaction usually starts with the usual sniffing and circling, then there will be manoeuvres to stay at the side or rear end, and – whoosh! – one dog gets his leg over.

In some cases he may have been a little more polite, trying a few miniaturised mock-ups – placing one paw on the rump or back, a small rise up, front feet off the ground – testing the water to find out what will be allowed. The other dog responds in a variety of ways, which may lead to the offending dog changing his strategy. Alternatively, the other dog may take it as a play invitation; he may flip around presenting his front end and face to the rear end focused dog, he may sit tight, or he may roll over on his back. He may have to keep repeating these behaviours over a period of time before the other dog is prepared to give up.

Intent on mounting the Dalmatian, the Collie type looks prepared to step his warning up with tense body and face. She has tried to flip around, but he is very determined.

THE EXTREME VERSION: "Oh, don't you like it?"

Insecure dogs, pushy dogs, and sex-driven dogs are the extremists in this scenario, and each will behave a little differently:

1. The insecure extremist: The root cause of his behaviour derives from being scared when severely told off by some other dogs. He now backs off if strongly told off. However, with dogs that try to get away, or are only giving mild warnings, he becomes even more intent on the job. It is fear that intensifies his behaviour.

2. The Pushy Dog: He is not quite so insecure and will go along with the other dog's response, but just won't give up: "You want to play or do flip-arounds? I will too, but at the first chance I will mount your back or your head!" If a warning is delivered he just ignores it, all he cares about is getting in a good position to mount. The challenge may even excite him further.

3. The sex-driven dog: The thought of sex makes for even greater persistence! Turbo-fuelled by hormones produced by a bitch coming in, or going out, of season, his behaviour becomes even more extreme. The result is that, unless the bitch is ready and receptive to being mated, her objections will go unheeded. The hormonally driven dog will pester her, ignoring all her polite requests and reasonable warnings until he forces her to use aggression. If she has had limited socialisation or is already a bit nervous, an aggressive response is a certainty.

5. "DON'T SNIFF ME THERE!"

When two dogs meet and sniff, one dog's body posture may be very upright as he investigates the other dog,

This Terrier tries to give a low level warning growl with lips forward. The loose tail and soft ears suggest he is not overly worried. If the larger dog doesn't back off, helping him out will prevent him from needing to escalate his warning.

ready to spring out of the way if he gets investigated around his private areas. Either in anticipation, or as the other dog sniffs, he may display a stiff stillness as an early warning. If the other dog continues his attentions, he may turn suddenly or spin or he may continually move away to keep his nether regions private.

THE EXTREME VERSION: "Don't even come near me!"

The extremist goes beyond bouncing and moving away; he doesn't want another dog anywhere near his personal space. He will air snap, bare his teeth, maybe growl and bark as he repeatedly darts – partially towards the other dog – then breaks away. This is a very clear warning that he doesn't want an intimate conversation.

6. "YEAH, YEAH – I'VE SEEN IT ALL BEFORE..."

When the novelty and excitement of meeting and playing with another dog is dwindling, this type of dog will just stand there while being investigated. He is putting up with the situation but he is keen to get on with 'his stuff' – sniffing and marking, hunting, playing with his owner or his known canine mates.

Hoping the Boxer will go away, the Retriever lies down in a non-threatening stance, freezing in position and not making eye contact. The Boxer cannot resist at least a sniff, but he politely stays a little back and reaches his head forward.

Many a dog who feels this way will continue to do his own thing, avoiding reciprocating unwanted attention. If he is worried about the meeting, you will see lots of visual checks even though he is keeping his nose down, and he may spend some significant time watching as the dog moves away. He will show much

more tension if the other dog does come to investigate. Often, though, other dogs don't bother with him – he looks boring!

THE EXTREME VERSION: "Let's stay out of it"

The extremist stance is: "I don't look, so therefore you can't be there". These are the toy-mad dogs, and the total avoiders.

"Let's play and let me focus on my toy so I don't have to interact with another dog – preferably ever!" This works, as it does for the dog who stays on the outskirts or ventures into the woodland to avoid contact. That is, until a keen dog seeks him out...This dog would probably choose to avoid dog parks.

7. "NICE TO MEET YOU – BUT PLEASE DON'T PUSH YOUR LUCK"

This reaction comes from meeting more extremists than relaxed, confident dogs, and may be felt by dogs who have had none or only a few interactions with new dogs. There is tension in the body and in the atmosphere. The dog's stance is very upright and forward, sniffing is delayed until the other dog has been checked for extremist tendencies. Hackles may be up, tail erect. If the other dog is not an extremist, the interaction might develop nicely depending on the reaction he gets.

The larger Terrier (pictured left) has tight, forward lips and lowered neck; he is warning the other terrier who seems to have stopped still. There is still lots of tension but neither wants to escalate the situation. They may get 'stuck' if neither has the confidence to leave.

THE EXTREME VERSION: "Actually, I am quite scared"

Meet other extremists, and the true colours of nervousness will show through. He will use 'stay away from me' strategies: perhaps a big, loud, startling, single woof, or a milder warning, such as going still. He may try something in between – going still, lifting his lips or growling.

This dog is a little too worried to use the pre-warning strategies of turning his head away or moving away, but he will not be drawn into a fight. He may sometimes go as far as an aggressive display – lasting 1-5 seconds – with lots of air snapping and snarling, but rarely making contact.

HELP OUT!

If he meets another "please don't push your luck" dog, the pair can get stuck with neither wanting to risk leaving. Try to keep initial meetings brief. Having practised recalling him away for a treat or to walk on, use that strategy now to help out so that your dog does not escalate his stay-away strategies to a more proactive, aggressive defence.

8. "LET'S GET OUT OF HERE QUICKLY"

This dog is highly stressed but he may appear to be faultless in his interactions so, for his owner, he isn't an obvious problem. In situations where he is unlikely to meet another dog he will sniff more, walk in a more casual fashion and toilet. But when he is likely to meet other dogs – in the park for example – he is constantly on the alert, worrying about potential meetings and greetings.

He dare not relax and take in his environment, and

The tense, upright posture of the Great Dane tells of his uncertainty. The Rottie softens his body language, turning and lowering his head.

will probably stick close to his owner. When he sees another dog he will do his best to avoid it, getting past as quickly as possible. When this is impossible he will freeze if investigated, scarcely checking out the other dog. The relief when that dog goes away is tangible: a shake, a sudden short spurt of movement, jumping up, grabbing at you, or maybe relieving himself. Then it's back to watch duty – and hoping that it won't be long before reaching the safety of the street or the car.

THE EXTREME VERSION: "There's a dog – I'm off!"
This is the dog that opts to run away rather than have another dog check him out. As he spots the interloper, he plans an escape route – and then he's off! If you are lucky enough to be in an area with lots of cover, he may find a place to hide, otherwise it's back to the car or home! This may be an inconvenience for you, but it's a traumatic experience for your dog.

HELP OUT!

Every time he runs away he thinks he has escaped a dog that would otherwise have attacked him. He desperately needs help to build his confidence. In the meantime, stay away from situations he may want to run from. To cope with other dogs is torture. By giving him no choice, the only strategy he is left with is to shut down – minimum movement, no attempts to communicate – becoming the equivalent of an object in order to survive the unwanted attentions. To force a dog to undergo this is cruelty. However, there are ways to make other dogs appear less traumatic for your dog. Until then, such experiences should be avoided.

9. "HE RAN – SO I CHASED"

This is such a hard one to be diligent about. This dog can meet lots of dogs without problems – it is only when the other dog is frightened that there is cause for concern. Even if the other dog is worried, as in the non-extremist versions of "Please be my friend?" or "Don't sniff me there!", all will be well as long as the other dog stands his ground.

But should he show any indication of moving away out of fear, he will become the target. The dog that chases is usually scared himself but, perhaps, feels more like a hero if he can get the other dog to run away from him. He is also able to make a clear distinction between frightened and appeasing dogs. The appeasing dog will back off and get out of his space, which is quite exciting to him. But the real fun is with frightened dogs. Now when he gives his dramatic lunge bark and bounce, he doesn't back off. He stays there so the other dog has to move away and, hopefully, runs, enabling the chase he desires. Being chased is very scary for the other dog. A particularly frightened dog can make illogical decisions, such as running into a tree or wall, running in the 'wrong' direction, across roads or through traffic. A chased dog easily becomes a lost dog or an accident statistic. For this reason, a chaser must be kept under control.

The lolloping canter of the leading Chihuahua tells us that this is a game and she trusts the incoming dog. Coming in low and fast, the long coated Chi makes a controlled grab with teeth covered.

THE EXTREME VERSION: "Go on – run"

He may have been frightened to begin with and opted for chasing the other dog away. But if he is allowed to practise, the thrill of the chase takes over and he becomes an addict. The fear element is minimal and because he learns to pick his victim carefully, confidence in this strategy grows quickly. The extremist is so high on chasing that he goes to greater and greater lengths to try and get the other dog to run. He charges up, he increasingly tries it with dogs that are not such easy targets and therefore he has to up this game with more barking, bouncing and lunging. He may even air snap or bump the other dog. He will be persistent and difficult to distract or to remove from the scene. He doesn't want a fight and mostly stays away from the face, but if this behaviour goes to its extreme he may try biting at the tail, rump or back legs of the runner. On catching him, he may even pin and stand over his victim and, even worse, he may attack. Attacks are unusual and killing is rare, but it does occasionally happen.

10. "I'M THE TOUGH GUY AROUND HERE – SEE!"

The dog that goes around with this sort of attitude is calm, cool, collected – and intimidating! Thankfully, these types are few in number. His movements are generally steady and calculated; he rarely rushes in but approaches in strident, forceful fashion. He is likely to put his head over the neck of the other dog. If the other dog drops, he will stand over or put a paw on him. If there is an outburst from the other dog, Mr Tough Guy holds his ground. He keeps his weight forward as he has no intention of backing off. If the other dog tries to warn him, he moves his head to safety but otherwise stays in position.

The female Mastiff runs in a playful manner – but play isn't the male's intention

Turning his face to avoid any potential telling off, he uses his weight through his shoulder to keep her down. You might just be able to see her lip lick, and behind her left paw is the tip of a tightly tucked tail.

He has his weight and elbow on her unprotected stomach. Submission is her only choice. There have been no aggressive signals but she is clearly being bullied.

Mr Tough Guy often gives little or no audible warnings. This, along with his calm demeanour and his ability to 'forget' and move on, often leads to the victim's owner apologising as they drag away their lunging, snarling dog who is desperately trying to keep Mr Tough Guy at bay. Mr Tough Guy is easily spotted by experienced dogs or dogs who have met him previously and now seek to avoid him. But, sadly, puppies, youngsters and naive dogs will seek interaction which results in a frightening often emotionally scarring experience.

THE EXTREME VERSION: "Bet you won't beat me!"
The extremist can lack the finesse of his counterpart. He has no interest in any conversation and immediately goes to fight mode. His approach may be just as controlled – and he may not even initiate any communication – but as he has less confidence in the outcome, he is quick to attack. The owner of this type of dog has a tough and lonely time of it, working out how to avoid interactions and trying to maintain control if the need arises.

It is tempting to try again to see if the extremist has learnt his lesson, maybe using a bite prevention measure such as keeping him muzzled. But such trials should not be undertaken with unsuspecting dogs you may encounter on walks. The risk of destroying another dog's emotional balance is too great. In this situation, you need to seek the help of a behaviourist who can plan and supervise interactions with other dogs.

COULDN'T CARE LESS – OR COULD HE?
Dogs that appear to tolerate extremists are often overlooked, but by focusing on their emotional state it will become obvious if they are uncomfortable.

Clues that happen during interaction:
- Use of avoiding body language.
- Lip lick flicks throughout.
- Sniffing with eyes focused elsewhere.
- Trying to take breaks.
- Arousal level – high – before, during and after.

Recovery signals on parting:
- Body shake off.
- Jumping up at you.

Both dogs are engaging in play, and might even be said to be mirroring – but they are not! The brindle dog holds his weight backwards, looks away, and shows tighter facial features. Creating a break might mean the brindle dog doesn't actually choose to return to 'play.'

- Marking, scratch backs.
- Slow to regain normal, exploratory behaviours.
- Easily aroused.

What may be a tolerable experience for one dog may be traumatic for another. For the traumatised dog, a single experience may be enough to convert him to use aggressive displays to keep other dogs away. Such aggressive displays also erupt when the initially tolerant dog eventually loses his patience.

There are consequences if your dog feels pestered:
- His trust in your ability to look after him will diminish.
- He will experience increasing ease of going to higher levels of aggressive display to make a point.

If your dog is being subjected to another dog's unwanted attentions and warnings are being ignored, you should intervene before more extreme behaviour becomes necessary. Bear in mind, an escalation to aggression can become the norm if the dog believes that warnings do not work.

WHAT CAN YOU DO?

DISTRACTING YOUR DOG

Employing techniques such as toy play and treat-giving to distract a worried dog from another dog can be a big help if the other dog is on-lead but when off-lead, it can make matters worse:

- Other dogs may come over, attracted by the toys and treats.
- Your dog gets a shock to find the other dog is right beside him.
- The problem – your dog is frightened of other dogs – therefore persists.

UNWANTED FRIENDS

- Don't compromise your dog by encouraging other dogs towards you with treats.
- If you do have an unwelcome tag-along, keep him away from your dog by body blocking and giving, or even throwing, treats, until the owner can get him.

MEETING EXTREMISTS

If the owner of an extremist dog controls him – keeping him calm and calling him away when necessary – meets and greets are mostly possible, as long as you:

- Follow the Hints and Tips: Avoiding problems (page 89).
- Insist on progressing at a rate that works for both dogs.
- Supervise interactions and be ready to intervene.

SO YOU OWN AN EXTREMIST?

The majority of dogs who behave in an extreme way when interacting with other dogs are, otherwise, great companions. But owning one of these dogs makes you very aware of the responsibility that is owed to the dog community around you. The extremists, if allowed to practise, are at risk of converting whole dog communities into suspicious on-guard canines – not something you want to be responsible for! All the time he is practising, he refines and perfects his anti-social skills – not something you want to develop.

Besides which, is it ever reasonable to walk an extremist in situations where other dogs are off-lead? Owners of extremists sometimes justify such a situation because they have their dog on-lead or muzzled, so they blame other dogs for approaching.

However, this is an abdication of responsibilities. It does no favours to either side and creates an emotional lose-lose situation.

The questions we should really be asking are:

- Is there a way I can be sure my dog will not emotionally or physically compromise another dog?
- Is there a way to prevent my dog's undesirable behaviour from occurring and, therefore, being repeatedly practised?
- How do I ensure each experience will nurture a sociable attitude towards other dogs?

For dogs that go straight into fight mode or who have bitten, chased, held or shaken another dog, a different strategy will need to be employed. Meeting and greeting will not be the initial aim. There will be substantial work to do to develop a positive and relaxed feeling simply on seeing another dog.

AVOIDING OTHER DOGS

If you cannot trust your dog to meet and greet other dogs, it is better to avoid them rather than causing untold damage.

To make this work for you and your dog:

- Allocate the time you would have spent walking your dog to playing, training and mentally stimulating your dog at home.
- Walk the streets at prime 'smell-time', i.e. sunrise and sunset.
- Find routes other dog walkers avoid, such as near the road when you are in open woodland or parkland.
- Shopping centre car parks, industrial estates and roadside verges can be very interesting places for your dog.
- Be prepared to walk in weather conditions that everyone else is avoiding!

IT'S NORMAL TO DISAGREE

Neither humans nor dogs are machines, we are all individuals with personal likes and dislikes, wants and needs and so, inevitably, there will be disagreements. In fact, a person that always complies with everyone else's interests, and does not have a mind of their own, might be regarded as weak and insipid. They are certainly highly vulnerable and need protection. Many people like nothing better than a good argument and, unfortunately there are a few who like nothing better than a good fight.

Mostly, in any given group, there are acceptable ways to express disagreement. These might vary a little from culture to culture, and even with a single person it might vary from work place to pub to home, but there is an unspoken agreement as to where the line is drawn. There is a fundamental knowledge of what is acceptable and what is not; what is considered polite or impolite. For dogs the same holds true. However, if we compare like for like – facial expression to facial expression, body language and gesture to body language and posture, verbal swearing and shouting to barking and growling – where the line is drawn is very different. 'Acceptable' and 'polite' in both species revolves around negotiation.

For dogs, snarls, growls and air-snaps are easily delivered and quickly recovered from. In dog parlance such communication is negotiation – it is perfectly acceptable and just about polite! Emotional injury hardly exists if we humans allow such communication and resist increasing arousal levels by our reactions.

ON-LEAD MEETINGS

Everything that happens in off-lead meetings and greetings can, in theory, also happen on-lead, albeit more clumsily with us in the way! Many dogs are very competent at meeting strange dogs while both are on-lead; in most training classes and dog sports this is the only way they do meet a new dog. However, complications arise for dogs that get frustrated or those who feel they cannot get away. Owners can use leads, collars and harnesses in a way that makes communication more difficult, and as always, previous on-lead experiences will have a great effect on how both you and your dog respond. To what extent your dog is keen to greet another dog on-lead will be dependent on four main factors:

- How your dog expects to greet others.
- How the other dog responds.
- What you have done in the past.
- What you do this time.

Being told off and then dragged into the other dog will do little to build this pup's confidence in his owner when on-lead around other dogs. The strangling slip lead will add further to the pup's distress.

FRUSTRATION

The first four categories of interaction are all open to frustration:

1. "Please be my friend?" Extremist: "Please, please, please be my friend"
2. "Shall we play?" Extremist: "I know you really want to!"
3. "You smell so interesting" Extremist: "Oh, I forgot you are a dog"
4. "I would just like to get my leg over" Extremist: "Oh, don't you like it?

For these dogs, being on-lead is a nuisance. It's probably like us trying to have a conversation when one person is outside the car and the other inside, with the window jammed tightly closed.

Yes, it's possible, but unless you compensate – speaking more slowly and enunciating the words – it is a frustrating experience. Something similar happens to dogs when they get frustrated on-lead – particularly the extremists. The whole communication thing breaks down and meetings often don't go as well as they would if they were off-lead (or the window was down!).

WHEN THE WORST HAPPENS, FOR YOUR DOG'S SAKE:

Helping Out

- Stay calm (avoid shouting at the other dog or his owner).
- Continue to walk on as if nothing significant has happened (unless the other dog is obviously injured or traumatised), and avoid checking your dog over immediately.
- Remind yourself that we humans are often more traumatised than the dogs are. Assess you dog's body language.

Strong pulling, lunging, up on hind legs, barking and high-pitched squeaking noises are all attempts to get access to the other dog. As an owner it seems obvious not to allow access, and it also seems obvious to use some form of correction. However, applying this can have unforeseen results and what was 'just' frustration becomes increasingly tinged with aggressive displays. By denying access, the root cause of his frustration is made greater and correction simply adds the emotion of fear to an already aroused dog.

The frustrated dog almost seems to forget about his original purpose and takes his frustration out on you, his lead or the other dog. Like anger management for humans, this dog needs help in dealing with his frustration. Repeatedly denying contact serves only to increase his frustration.

The more his focus is on getting to the dog rather than talking to him, the less well his attentions will be received. Other dogs' response will soon begin to change his view of them. If you cannot redirect his focus before the frustration arises, you should avoid restrictive lead situations for now. First work on regaining his focus in distracting situations which do not involve other dogs. Getting help with training in the early stages will prevent straightforward frustration tipping over into frustrated, aggressive displays.

THE OTHER DOG'S RESPONSE

When you sit down beside someone on a plane, how they respond hugely affects where you look, what you do, what you say and how you feel. If your fellow passenger smiles and nods at you, you will probably make eye contact and exchange a brief greeting or chat for a minute or two. You will sit down and position your whole body feeling more at ease than if your companion had given a big sigh, avoided looking at you, and repositioned themselves, moving and turning their body away from where you are about to sit.

What if you are about to sit in your allocated seat and your neighbour-to-be glares at you, swears about the situation and keeps his arm over both arm-rests? What do you say? How do you sit down? How do you feel? The response of the other person (or dog) is everything. In all but the most extreme of the extremists, response has a huge impact on the level of arousal, expectation, and the chosen course of action.

TWO NERVOUS DOGS MEET...

Upright and tense the nervous Tibetan Terrier and appeasing Border Collie meet.

When the Collie is called away for a break, the Tibetan seizes the opportunity for a sneaky sniff.

Their body language is more relaxed in this re-meet, only seconds later.

The immediate marking on parting is a clue to the relief experienced.

For example:
- A bouncy, playful dog, giving lots of invites, may be quite tempting to some, but overwhelming for others.
- A calmer dog, giving soft body language with perhaps an occasional play invite, is certainly worth talking to.
- A dog that just carries on sniffing is probably quite safe – but not worth bothering with.

ON-LEAD MEET-UPS

KIT
If you dog's body language is altered by pulling on the lead – either you pulling him back from a dog, or when he pulls to get at a dog – not only will he feel compromised, the other dog will get a distorted message. This is particularly exaggerated when a short lead or a head halter are used. Try a long lead, approximately 2m (6ft) in length, which allows for flexibility.

YOUR END OF THE LEAD
When you meet another dog:
- Rather than pull your dog to you, work down the lead as you continue to walk.
- Keep the two leads from tangling by maintaining 6 o' clock and 12 o' clock positions with the dogs at the centre of the clock.
- Hold the lead so that it is neither taut nor slack; if anything happens there will be no snatch/yank or risk of lead tangle.

When you are holding your dog on a lead, you are inclined to be more aware of his behaviour than the other dog's demeanour. Owners of dogs who have just started using aggressive displays can often be confused as to why their dog can sometimes be aggressive, and sometimes not. This is because the way the other dog reacts will influence your dog: where he looks, how he moves, what he says, and very much how he feels: excited, pleased, worried, frightened or relaxed. When holding that lead, meeting other dogs doesn't take two, it takes three... actually it takes four – the other owner, too. No wonder it's so much more complicated than off-lead meetings.

WHAT ARE YOU DOING?
What you say to your dog, how you say it, by what piece of kit (collar, harness, etc.) you are connected and how you hold it, will all be influencing how your dog feels and therefore how he will greet and interact with the other dog. Given that most dogs are much better communicators off-lead, we want to simulate this as far as possible.

BECOMING MORE FAMILIAR
Meeting the same dogs again and with repeated meet ups, will result in changes in the way the dogs communicate – generally interaction is less urgent and less intrusive. Owners will also be more relaxed knowing how the dogs are likely to behave. It is easy to conclude that your dog will approach a dog he has never encountered before in the way he meets and greets those he has previously met – but he won't. It is as different as you meeting your friends down the pub compared to being interviewed for a new job. Your young dog needs to regularly meet new non-extreme dogs if you want his interview skills to stay top notch. He needs practice in the flexibility and caution necessary when first encountering a new dog.

Meeting dogs he already knows is so much less arousing. The energy expended does not create the

These puppies probably had a disagreement during play; both have their teeth covered not wanting to terminate the interaction. There was probably quite a bit of vocalisation, which would be a further clue that this is all about warnings, not about fighting.

same intensity – yes, there may be lots of excitement – especially if it progresses to play. But even then the speed and anticipation is reduced; it happens simply from getting to know what each other will do or won't do, and the ability to break away from each other will happen more easily. After a few play meets, dogs beyond adolescence may not even bother to play anymore, or only occasionally – the predictability score seems to reduce the need to play. For the youngster, however, the play may be addictive. The moment your dog detects his best friend is in the vicinity he will be intent on finding him, anticipating the high-energy play that will ensue. Be aware the ease with which you can be totally obliterated from your dog's mind – and be warned that it can take a lot of work to change this way of thinking.

Re-meets for some dogs will have the positive impact of reducing the need to check each other out. The urgency to meet will be gone; they may not even appear to sniff each other at all – but keep your eyes open for them sniffing the air or where they have rolled, eaten grass or urinated.

Alternatively, the sniffing may be so brief and casual that their heart rate has probably stayed the same as before they spotted each other. A complete absence in awareness of each other is rare, even if they appear to be taking no notice of each other. Watch where the dog's eyes are looking, even if his head is not pointing in that direction.

Watch, too, for that nose quivering to catch the scent on the wind, or investigating the air scent after the two dogs have passed each other. It seems a bit like us, in a public place, taking sneaky peeks at someone we hardly know when they are looking elsewhere. You want to find out a bit more about them but you don't want the pressure of a conversation.

FROM ENEMY TO ASSOCIATE!

Where there was an initial meeting with aggressive warnings, avoidance behaviours may be exaggerated

Peacekeeping: The longer coated Collie (left) is focused on the stick he is about to steal. The other Collie (right), with ears held back, is not going to mount a challenge – he does a deflecting, grooming lick at the other Collie's eyes. Look at his whiskers pointing fully forward, sensing the exact whereabouts of the stick thief! Both dogs are comfortable with this 'peace' protocol – there is no tension or any overt avoidance behaviour.

with the head turning away, and moving in a deliberate fashion to increase the distance. As this acknowledgement of each other gets repeated successfully it will get less exaggerated, as the two dogs trust that neither is intending to threaten the other. Even dogs that have previously had a brief fight will often re-meet using dramatic body language only at a warning level, and part company without taking it to a fight ever again. However if one of the dogs is on our extremist list, he will need his owner's help to prevent the interaction escalating in the wrong direction.

By understanding both dogs, it will be easier to know how much help they need in order to develop successful long-term tolerance of each other. But because only a few dogs want to fight, this is much more achievable than owners often think. You can help out by taking the re-meet very slowly, and creating and supporting the dogs' options to avoid each other. This action can achieve 'park-worthy' results.

It never ceases to fascinate me how well dogs remember each other. After one or two meetings, from henceforth, it will be obvious they have previously met. Even if it was a year or so ago, even if they have been trimmed from a ball of fluff that was hard to tell head from tail into a skinny posh Poodle that you might not recognise – they recognise each other!

The dog recognition part of their brains must be full of different scent patterns for each dog, whereas our person- recognition is much more like a visual photo library. We can, initially, be thrown by a change in weight or hairstyle, whereas dogs may be confused by changes in scent patterns. For example, a dog that has been neutered several months previously may be initially approached as a stranger; a dog with a metabolic illness, or who has been staying in kennels or on a completely different diet may be momentarily inspected as if he is a new dog. The visual appearance is identical – but the smell... What a different world theirs is to ours!

SUMMING UP

Each dog has a regularly-used pattern of behaviour on meeting other dogs. The majority of socially adept dogs who display these patterns will fit into one of the categories discussed. However, at the extreme of each of these categories, less social dogs exist (here called 'extremists').

Many features affect how smoothly these meetings go including:
- Previous experiences.
- If they have met before – even once or twice.
- Pre-existing state of arousal.
- Environmental distractions.
- Speed of the meeting.
- On-lead meetings – there are four factors to take into consideration: two dogs and two people.

With dogs that struggle, slowing down the meeting process has the biggest impact on their acceptance of each other. Think scent, then sight and – only when the intensity has dropped – progress to contact. Frustration is easily misread as early aggression but, dealt with sensitively, it need not tip in that direction. Showing teeth, growling, air snapping – even a forward lunging and barking outburst – are only warnings. They are not evidence of intent to injure.

"Let them sort it out themselves" is only an appropriate management technique for non-extremists. It otherwise allows bullies to perfect their undesirable skills, and pushes victims to become defensive or shut down.

Observe your dog. Not all dogs that:
- Engage in play are happily consenting.
- Rush up to meet a new dog would choose to even meet if the process was slowed down.

Be comfortable about protecting your dog around extremists. Equally, extremists need to be managed to ensure good experiences both for themselves, and for the wider dog community

Chapter Nine

STRANGER DANGER!

The human/canine clash

Your dog is an integral member of the family circle; you therefore want him to be with you as much as possible. You have a relationship with him in the home, in more formal environments, such as at a training club or at a competition, and on walks. But what happens when he meets or passes by people he doesn't know? What sort of a relationship does he develop with them? How do you expect him to react? As usual, we tend to have unrealistically high expectations and, what makes it even more difficult, the behaviour we want either makes very little sense to our dogs or is entirely contradictory:

We want a dog who will, for example:

- Protect us from anyone who looks suspicious – but not to bark at 'odd' looking people (e.g. in fluorescent work wear, wearing a big, floppy hat, using a walking frame).
- Protect us from people behaving aggressively towards us – but not to react when a long lost friend runs across the street with arms outstretched.
- Be friends with everyone – but to pay no attention to non-doggy people.
- Greet doggy people – but not to jump up and slobber when they are wearing smart clothes.
- Allow a toddler to grab him and pat him on the head – but not clean the ice cream from their face.
- Get out of the way so you don't trip over him – but stay still when someone steps over him in the pub.
- Move when you push him off the bed – but stay still when the vet pushes and prods him during an examination.

How your dog responds in any of these situations is a product of both genetics and upbringing. In terms of breed or breed type some breed standards actively promote and encourage traits such as being "reserved', "wary" or "watchful" of strangers. Any dog with this wired into his genetic make-up is predisposed to be in a state of stress when meeting strangers, and may even attempt to avoid them altogether. Their body language and communication signals will reflect their fear or

Early Experiences

This pup is a bit worried as the strangers approach, but a surge of confidence as they pass triggers a chase behaviour, often seen in the herding and terrier breeds. If this pup is allowed to practise this behaviour, it could develop into a chasing problem. He needs more time to investigate and get to know a person – and then leave before they do.

even the more proactive version of fear – aggression. We also know their early interactions with the breeder, watching how their mother reacts to people, plus their experiences during early socialisation will all contribute to how they respond to a stranger as an adult.

WHO IS A STRANGER?

To you or me it's people who pass us by on the street or the road, those we have not either previously met or those we know nothing about. However, someone who we know about through our general knowledge or whom we are aware of through friends or family, such as the shopkeeper or our child's teacher, is not a stranger to us – even on a first meeting. For your dog it cannot be reasoned out like this. He must rely on experience to work out who is a stranger and who is not, and he will not regard frequency of encounters to be the only determining factor. In a dog's mind, familiarity does not necessarily mean acceptance.

Your dog may have met a particular person on many occasions but still regards them as suspicious or to be avoided. Equally, he may meet someone else for the first time and show relaxed body language in their presence. Each dog will have his own threshold of when a stranger becomes a friend and although for the dog there is a consistency, acceptance will vary from stranger to stranger. There is also a pattern in what may appear unpredictable. Some owners will have had sufficient negative experiences to adopt a policy of trying to avoid encounters with strangers because they know their dog will find it difficult and stressful, or they find their dog's reaction embarrassing.

Others take a more blasé approach saying of their dog: "he doesn't mind", "he's alright", "ignore his barking, he's fine". But watch the body language; the dog may seem OK but what is he really feeling? If you observe closely, you will be able to make an informed assessment and, hopefully, this will give you the understanding to take supportive action if necessary. So how does your dog feel about people other than those he lives with? What does his body language tell you about his underlying emotions?

"HOW EXCITING – A NEW PERSON!"

For this dog there will be lots of tail wagging, perhaps jumping up, squeaking and barking – the dog is more

Seeing this scenario, it's easy to think that the dog enjoys saying hello. But let's take a look at the more subtle body language before and during the meeting.

BEFORE: Only a moment earlier, the dog turned his head and body away and stood still, telling us of his uncertainty. The swishing tail tells us he is aroused by the stranger's excitement. Given a choice, he would not seek interaction.

DURING: The dog initiates contact, and he moves into the stranger, seeming to enjoy the attention. However, his tail is tightly clamped over his anus, and he is focused on his owner. This is the same look children give their parents when they don't want to be parted from them. Although he engages with the stranger, emotionally he wants to be with his owner.

interested in getting a response from the stranger than having a sniff. Owners variously describe their dogs' behaviour when greeting strangers as:

- An over-the-top greeting.
- A bark and greet (often with wriggly bodies).
- A licky, roll on the back greeting.

These different forms of behaviour give vital clues as to how the dog regards the stranger. There is undoubtedly lots of excitement – but what else is going on?

OVER-THE-TOP GREETINGS

When your dog is off lead, does he rush off to say hello to anyone he meets within the vicinity? This would be typical of a young, excitable Labrador Retriever who forgets all about you when there is a new person in the area. He charges up, front legs braking on the stranger's body with his tail wagging furiously. He repeatedly jumps on and off, and is deaf to your calls. In all the excitement, he cannot pay attention to anything else. The dog who gives this high-energy greeting is usually oblivious to the recipient's response; in his initial outburst he scarcely notices whether his greeting is being returned or not. When the high-energy greeter is lead walking, he is constantly looking to see if anyone is approaching.

The moment a person approaches, he actively seeks eye contact and as soon as he gets it, the energy level increases. He pulls towards the stranger, with circular tail wagging, often bouncing and head nodding or doing partial play bows until he makes contact – unless you manage to drag him past! As with an off-lead greeting, he will attempt to jump up and will repeat the on/off behaviour.

These high-energy greeters are supremely unaware of everything else that is going on when they are intent on greeting someone. However, if the owner has used punishing or startling techniques or has been effective with verbal reprimands ("off"/"down"), there will be another change in behaviour. You will see appeasement type behaviours creeping in – the dipped neck, and increased focus on trying to get to the face and particularly the mouth. Unfortunately, the intensity and duration of the whole display is increased, even if the jumping is reduced.

1. This Border Collie has jumped up to greet, but everything about his face is tense, his eyes engage but he pulls his head back and turns away.

2. He licks at the stranger's face as he, appeasingly, lowers his tense rear end.

3. Mounting the stranger is even a consideration in his conflicted state. Certainly he is excited and, certainly, he wants to make contact with the stranger. However, these displacement behaviours arise from a lack of confidence in interacting. Unfortunately such behaviours are encouraged by well-intentioned people.

The high-energy greeter may be full of good intentions, but his behaviour is unacceptable. The young and the frail cannot cope with these over-the-top greetings, and they are alarming for those who are wary of dogs. You may have started using excuses saying: "he's just being friendly", but after a few encounters with unimpressed strangers, outings become as stressful as if you were coping with an aggressive dog. To avoid serious problems, the high-energy greeting needs to be managed or, at the very least, redirected. You need to make sure:

- He meets lots of new people but finds them less interesting than you.
- Ensure all these people ignore him or do not encourage him to interact.
- Resist mirroring his high arousal or fast, extravagant movements by remaining calm and using slow and gentle body movements.
- Become an easy access treat dispenser when new people are around, delivering treats before, during and after any possible encounter (see panel opposite).
- Build up your relationship through play and training games.

BARK AND GREET

(Also see The "give me space" dog, page 108).

Many of the guarding breeds and many of the small breeds will be excited and keen to meet a stranger – but there is also some initial barking. This happens

TREATS VERSUS STRANGER

Your dog may be a real foodie at home or in other situations where he feels relaxed, but how can you ensure that he focuses on the treats when all his focus is on a potentially exciting meeting?

- Smelly, juicy food is likely to be of greater value than commercial dog treats.
- Get your dog 'into' his special treats before you encounter a person.
- Take the treats to his nose when he can see, but isn't near the person.
- Slowly toss the treat slightly above and, in front, of his gaze. You want the treat to land about 30cm (1 ft) in front of him – he won't be able to resist the movement
- Be generous and quick at delivering the treats.

Initially, you need to reward for even half a second's attention if he turns and looks at you, expecting a treat.

most particularly when there is a group of dogs and, certainly, the warning bark alerts everyone to the presence of the stranger. When on-lead or with a more confident dog, this type of behaviour will happen less or will be in a subdued form; the bark will be more sing-songy or with some breeds typically howly.

There may be some residual purpose to this noisy greeting although for some dogs it is simply "when

Alarm is evident in this dog's face – note the intense eyes and flared nostrils. However, the covered teeth and forward lips tell us there is no intention to attack.

Don't try pushing this one! The weaponry is on display for a reason.

This is a greeting bark. The dog doesn't even line up his body, which carries none of the tension seen in the other two photos. His eyes are soft and his lips are pushed forward.

I'm excited, bark" – and that's all there is to it. To any dog-wise person there is no aggression or overt fear in this greeting, though if you look more closely you may see that these barkers and greeters are also showing a degree of appeasement or avoidance. The dog may have a lowered body posture, he may back away avoiding physical contact, or he may bounce back and forth, his tail going in circles, wanting to be greeted but maybe not as confident as you originally thought. These appeasement behaviours often disappear after 5-10 seconds – perhaps the dog has made an assessment and has gained the necessary confidence?

MANAGING MEETINGS

Dogs who struggle with interactions can be helped by breaking up the greeting into small chunks:

Get in with the treats before your dog is first aware of the stranger. This will keep his arousal low and will help you to break up the meeting process:

- Have a look – give three treats (one immediately after the other..
- Have another look – have three treats.
- Have a few seconds to approach/sniff – have three treats.

You can give extra help and support by:

- Allowing on-lead greeting only, to start with.
- Using a lead to guide your dog's front feet back on to the ground.
- Providing extra special treats.
- Taking the treat to your dog's nose to lure him away (if necessary).
- Allowing your dog to sniff a personal possession (e.g. a glove) before meeting the actual person when you have visitors to the house.
- Making sure a treat always come from you when your dog has turned away from the stranger.

THE APPEASERS

These dogs – the 'wriggly gigglies' – are keen and excited to greet but appeasing behaviour dominates. The spine is lowered and almost gyrates, and the dog gives a full body wag. As the stranger approaches to make contact, one of two things may happen. The dog may collapse on the floor, going on one side but usually on his back, or he may make frantic efforts to get to

the stranger's face. Dog friendly strangers often find these behaviours irresistible: "ahh, he wants his tummy rubbed" or "he wants to kiss me". However, we need to look at the intensity of the behaviours before making a judgement. The dog has thrown himself on his back and is holding his tail and his limbs tight; his head and neck are tense and positioned looking away from the stranger. The 'kissy' dog is moving with great speed; his spine is lowered, his head is dipped in his shoulders, and there is a desperate quality to his behaviour.

1. The stranger would see the body tension and the head clamped to the ground, but we get the better view of her face. Her usually floppy face is held so tensely it easily defies gravity.

2. Her owner tries to roll her back on to her feet, but her desperation to prostrate herself is stronger. Her eyes stay fixed on the stranger.

3. With the stranger further away, she now has a chance to breathe. The physical exertion of holding herself so tensely, and the emotional stress, mean that panting is inevitable.

Both types of dog are appeasing and asking the stranger for acceptance. Their lack of confidence and trust drives them to make sure that they cannot be perceived as a threat: "here is my vulnerable stomach", or resorting to wolf cub, juvenile behaviour: "I will lick all round your mouth". In fact, both dogs need the stranger to back off as such attention increases their need to appease. If the stranger won't ignore your dog (i.e. not look, talk or touch), adopt the same strategy as for the bark and greet dog, but be quick to guide him back to you (with lead and treat) as soon as you can.

With this type of behaviour the less it is practised, the less likely it is to become ingrained. Therefore it is better if the stranger does not bend down and rub the dog's tummy but, rather, stands up and walks backwards, waits for the dog to stand and then rubs him under the chin or pets him in a way that encourages a confident posture. Equally, the stranger should keep their face away from the 'kisser', and fuss the dog at more of a distance. In fact, it may even be better to refrain from fussing altogether until the dog feels more comfortable and does not need to appease.

A teeth display with a breathy hiss – often called a smile – is another form of appeasement. If it is read in isolation, and the rest of the dog's body language is not taken into account, it may be interpreted as aggression.

1. This Collie cross with her head held high, out-stretched neck and tightly tucked rear end, is very appeasing. She goes into a lowered position, ready to roll over, in case of a perceived increase in pressure. Note the hand over the dog's head.

2. With this stranger, the head position looks less tense. She creeps closer, seeking more contact, but her back legs get left behind. Although her tail is looser than the previous photo, her rear end is still tucked. Note the hand under the dog's chin.

URINATION ON GREETING

This is the extreme version of rolling over on to the back, and is called submissive urination. It is, indeed, a very submissive gesture, more often seen in young dogs but also in older dogs when they are desperately trying not to present a challenge to another dog or human. The urination may happen when the dog is on his back, or more often when he is in a sitting position – often squatting lower than if he was relieving himself naturally. This behaviour applies to both male and female dogs. The rest of the body language is highly appeasing, with lots of squirming and creeping. Of course the dog is excited, but he is also frightened. He desperately needs you to slow down the meeting or manage the situation (see page 105) with the stranger ignoring him until he is more relaxed.

FREEZERS AND LEANERS

Not quite so extreme in energy are the freezers and leaners. Again, this greeting may be misread. A dog who is blasé and comfortable may also lean, but his behaviour is soft and relaxed and he doesn't do this at 'exciting' times. The worried dog, however, will hold his muscles taut and will appear tall with his head up, even though he is leaning into you. It may be that he is standing or sitting, or he may jump up against you. There may be a total freeze, a momentary freeze or a stilling of movement. He may close his mouth – holding, or partially holding his breath. In this scenario, the dog will not casually move out of the freeze. Commonly, as the stranger backs off, the dog suddenly leaps up towards their face, banging chin, nose or glasses, or there may be a sudden dash back to the owner or a mad five minutes as the dog rushes round and round as he experiences an overwhelming sense of relief.

A stranger may be lured into fussing and cuddling this type of dog as this seems to be what he is asking for, and the owner may well be proud of the dog's 'sociable' behaviour. But there are three clear indicators that show this is not the case; in fact, there is a significant element of fear. The signs to look for are:

- Body tension
- Breath held
- Relief outbursts at the end of the initial contact

The best scenario for the dog is for the stranger to back away and avoid bending over or touching him. The dog should be given a chance to relax before there is any attempt to make contact. If he is showing signs of doing so and is still seeking contact, a gentle tickle under the chin or a rub on his nearside ear or neck area will be more than enough – any more and you risk driving him back to his earlier state.

WHY IS THIS DOG FRIGHTENED?

If no one has ever hurt your dog and a stranger has never done anything bad to him, why should he be frightened? The answer is straightforward: it is because he is a dog who for whatever reason (genetic, familial or breed trend, or accrued experiences), feels the need to appease people. In effect he is saying: "Please be nice to me, please don't attack me, please, please, please…" How does the stranger respond? By stooping down towering over the dog, patting his head, rubbing his exposed tummy, looking at him directly in the face, all the time saying: "Oh, isn't he sweet…"

All the dog's efforts to get the stranger to lessen contact have had the opposite effect. So what else can he do? From his viewpoint there is only one option: to beg, beg, beg you to back off by being even more appeasing. Unfortunately, most people do not read it this way, and simply renew their efforts to make friends. It may be that the dog has never been exposed to cruel treatment from a stranger but, for the highly appeasing dog, it's a bad experience every single time a stranger makes close contact with him. He shouts it in

his body language: "please back off" but these people just keep coming. The dog is caught in an impossible situation, which he finds confusing and deeply stressful.

It is only by protecting the appeasing dog from unwelcome overtures that you can build his confidence and bring about a change in his behaviour. Bear this in mind when you are the 'stranger' meeting a dog of this type; you need to give him space so that his appeasing behaviours do not increase and intensify. Allow him to blossom emotionally; don't reinforce his servitude – let the dog be!

THE "PLEASE DON'T!" DOG
Please don't talk to me
Please don't come towards me
Please don't try and pet me

The dog who is trying to communicate these wishes is not aggressive and is rarely labelled as fearful but, in short, he would be much happier if he was ignored. If an experienced, well-socialised dog was meeting him, he would get the response he wanted. The other dog would read all the body language that he is supplying and would take the appropriate course of action – to ignore him. It would be nice to think that we could be sensitive enough to do the same. Maybe if you own a dog like this, you could convey his feelings to those who meet him or, at the very least, don't force him into accepting attention from strangers. The level of discomfort this dog is experiencing is not so extreme as to warrant an aggressive display or for him to run away, but he is not able to relax and enjoy contact with strangers. It is in this situation you will see a lot of calming signals – licking lips, yawning, head turning, scratching. There are also the big, geographical positioning behaviours which often get him into trouble:

- He can't come directly to you when you call because you are too near or talking to a stranger.
- There's a stranger between you and your dog so he comes slowly or arcs around the stranger, seemingly wasting time.
- He swaps sides as you walk along the road to create more space between himself and the approaching stranger.

- You ask your dog to "say hello", but he hangs back and ignores the stranger, sometimes 'chancing' to find an interesting smell on that wall or in that hedge, hoping he will be ignored.
- He acts the wimp and moves backwards or even hides behind you, effectively removing himself from the situation.
- As you pass a stranger, the dog pulls on the lead with the simple intention of getting past more quickly.

It seems strange that these behaviours are often 'corrected' or not allowed. When rehabilitating dogs that have previously lunged, barked and snapped at strangers, it takes a lot of carefully structured sessions to gradually build confidence and make more positive associations with people. When a dog eventually displays these "don't want to get involved" behaviours, it is a cause for celebration.

He is now using non-aggressive behaviours, doing what he did before his behaviour escalated and he felt the need to use defensive, aggressive behaviour. Watch closely and support the avoiding strategies – in this way your dog can trust you to protect him and he won't need to resort to more extreme behaviour. Another strategy for avoiding contact is the dog that turns away when a stranger comes near him, but sill keeps the person within his peripheral vision. When there is a visitor, the dog will settle himself in a position where he can still keep his eyes and ears easily orientated in the visitor's direction – he needs to know where they are and what they might do. On a walk he may appear to be sniffing the environment, but his eyes keep checking the whereabouts of the stranger.

There are dogs who don't want contact but who are less likely to move away. In this scenario, a dog will show lots of body tension, movement will be stiffer, ears will be back, and he will stare back if eye contact is made. If a hand is offered, he will dip his head to avoid it or go very still in a mild version of a freeze. His mouth will be tense and if he is panting, he will close his mouth, often appearing to hold his breath. He may blink or stare. When the stranger backs away, there is often a softening of body tension, a sigh or body shake off and, at that stage, the dog may feel confident enough to move away. In order to understand how the dog is feeling, you only have to put yourself in the same situation – someone invading your personal space, and not backing off when a request is made very clearly.

THE "GIVE ME SPACE" DOG

There is another scenario where the dog is desperately trying to increase distance between himself and the stranger, without making an obvious move. This is the scared – possibly extremely scared – dog that is doing all he can to get his message across without an overt display. The dog that feels able to move away adopts a lowered body posture, with ears tightly pinned. His movement is very controlled, almost stiff, and some dogs may appear to almost tiptoe away. In this instance, the dog's footfall on a floor surface will be much quieter than normal foot placing.

The dog will always know exactly where the stranger is; he will be watching and listening, and any sign of movement will be closely monitored. A sneeze or a sudden movement will cause the dog to startle. If approached, the dog will go very still – standing or lying with muscles tensed. Generally the head will be lowered and the facial muscles will be very tight. If the stranger continues to try to make contact, you will see a quiver of the upper lip, in the vein of a snarl; there may even be a low, rumbling growl with the mouth closed. The not-so-brave may crumble into a very tense, submissive roll over or may hunch up, which may be accompanied by submissive urination or emptying of the anal glands.

This is the limit of the dog trying to keep someone at a distance while still not doing anything proactive. He is using all the polite strategies available to ask for more space. If your dog is doing this, you must listen – he is desperate for your help. He needs you to get him out of a situation that he is too frightened to deal with. He goes into a freeze or gets stuck in a position because he is so polite. He is doing everything in his power to stop the situation from escalating. He is trying as hard as he can to avoid going up to the next level which involves actively sending the stranger away.

In this situation you should celebrate how wonderful your dog is, how hard he tries to avoid being aggressive – and for goodness' sake, help him out! Again observation is key. By watching his body language closely, you will be able to work out what his critical distance is when a stranger is in the vicinity.

1. Hunched up, with lowered neck and looking away, this Lurcher doesn't want to make contact.

2. Given a choice, she wants to create more distance.

3. When she perceives the threatening behaviour has ceased, she chooses to investigate the stranger.

There will be a measurable distance where he will swap from "life's ok" to: "oh, no, a stranger might be coming to get me". This gives a clear indication of how far away you should allow the dog to be. Confidence will grow and progress will be faster if the dog is just on the edge of his comfort zone – where he still feels secure enough not to start the "please back off'" behaviours.

There are a number of factors that may affect this critical distance, depending on the individual dog. For example, the distance may need to be greater if the stranger is wearing a hat or a fluorescent jacket, whether it is a tall man, or whether there are children. More often it is influenced by movement: the stranger running and advancing in your direction, or making quick, excited, or unpredictable movements. The distance will be less if the dog is otherwise feeling relaxed, and greater if he is stressed or highly aroused for other reasons.

You may think an urban situation would be more stressful for a dog who is worried by strangers – and for some it is, and they will shut down – but this is not always the case. The critical distance can reduce when you are continually going past people who never make contact, and be greater when walking along a quiet road where the presence of a stranger is more salient. Get into the habit of clocking the situation, then monitoring and responding appropriately according to the dog's response, making sure you take action at the earliest sign. Everything about your body language has to be relaxed and casual. If you talk to your dog, you should sound jolly and upbeat not cooing and reassuring.

Don't be tempted to let a stranger use treats to lure the dog to come in closer. If his body language shows he is scared – ears down, body tense, weight backwards, and stretching his neck to get to the treat – then he is. A treat will not take the fear away; only being at a safe distance and strangers who do not put pressure on him, will do that. You, the owner, might give him a treat when he is showing more comfortable body language with you, but don't force him into to the dilemma of putting himself in 'danger' in order to get a tasty treat (see page 112).

If a stranger is advancing, use your body and hands to block them from making contact with your dog. Keep your voice quiet and calm and politely ask the stranger who, doubtless, "loves all dogs" to look away and not talk to your dog. If the stranger takes this on board, you may well find your dog is able to go over and sniff him – which should be regarded as an

WHAT IS YOUR DOG'S CRITICAL DISTANCE

Watch your dog closely and work out how far away he is when:
• He has to keep his eyes on the stranger.
• His body becomes stiffer.
• His walking pace alters in speed, direction or fluidity.
• He does a lip lick.
• Ceases sniffing, or continues with a watchful eye.

Take on board these observations and move back so you are just within his comfort zone.

honour bestowed! If you don't get a positive response from the stranger, take your dog away. Who cares if you are accused of being a bit anti-social? Remember, this is your dog, and his emotional responses are in your hands. How real is the danger that your dog so clearly perceives? We do not know what he is thinking, but his body language is the same as if he knew, from prior experience, that another dog was going to attack him. It is more than likely that these dogs genuinely believe they are in danger of being attacked by strangers. Looking at the encounter from a dog's perspective:

The stranger stares at the dog, out of interest, or with the intention of saying hello.
The dog reads the stare as a threat.

The stranger comes closer intending to greet.
The dog perceives the threat closing in on him.

The stranger reaches a hand out to allow/encourage the dog to investigate.
The dog sees a weapon being aimed at him.

The stranger goes to pat the dog on the head.
The dog knows he is being attacked.

The dog has screamed "please back off" – but we humans just keep on coming, oblivious to the dog's attempts at peace negotiation. A literal example of blind ignorance.

MORPHING OF HUMANS

It is obvious when a dog has problems with meeting strangers, but what is going on in his head? How does he perceive the human race? His impressions may be less favourable if he has experienced the following innocent, maybe even well intentioned, interactions:

- Scary games which may include rough play or chase games.
- Handling or examination when he's been in pain.
- Physical or verbal correction.
- Witnessing a verbal outburst directed at others.
- Being close to someone during a traumatic experience.

PLAY AS A DIVERSION STRATEGY WITH STRANGERS

When this dog plays with his owner there is a softness in his movements.

On meeting a stranger, by way of displacement, he attempts to turn a worrying encounter into play – but the tension in his face and body is very different.

The dog morphs these reactions on to other people he may encounter. He brings the emotions he has experienced to these new interactions and behaves accordingly.

WHEN YOU ARE THE STRANGER

How should you respond to the dog that is shouting "don't come near me", or to the dog that is apparently or genuinely guarding his owner. First and foremost, if you are the stranger do not take any risks. With every single dog that has ever bitten, there was a first bite. There was a bite when the owner said "he's never done that before" – and he hadn't. Use distance, create barriers, take time to make sure you are not the first victim.

Strategies to adopt when meeting an unknown dog:

* Be careful about how you behave, and how your body language may be perceived. To a scared dog, it may appear threatening.
* Avoid direct approach cues – keep eyes, face, and shoulder pointing away from the dog. Even looking or talking to the nearby owner can be construed as a threat.
* Move with soft, fluid body movements, on the slow side, but certainly not stiffly or excitedly.
* If and when the dog stops barking, and if he is showing an interest, let him sniff your personal belongings. If appropriate, let him approach and check you out. Keep your body relaxed and avoid making contact with him. Avoid inviting him with out-stretched hand or patting your thigh. Crouching down can also be challenging.

Dogs showing any degree of avoidance, uncertainty or conflicted behaviours will appreciate this approach. For the majority of dogs, curiosity will outweigh any concerns they may have – especially if we allow them to behave as a dog. Investigating via sniffing is central to how dogs would like to start a conversation, be it with a new dog or a new person.

If you allow this to happen, the ensuing 'conversation' will be significantly more relaxed, evidenced by the dog's body language.

TREATING DANGER

Should you give the stranger treats? Absolutely not, or at least not until the dog's body language is relaxed, with nothing tense - ears relaxed, mouth soft, possibly open, body long, soft and fluid.

If you are giving treats to a dog who is still frightened and preparing to get away, i.e. body language tense and body weight backwards not neutral, and he's stretching forwards to take the treat, you are kidding yourself if you think the dog has accepted you. Being close does not mean he feels good about you or himself. You need to work on his emotional state, not the physical distance.

The same applies to dropping treats for a non-barking, scared dog. Do not try to get the dog closer to you – it does not help the dog relax. If you must give treats, wait until the dog is beginning to show relaxed body language, gently throw them so that you repeatedly cause the dog to create distance from you. If you have not previously used treats for distance decreasing, you will be surprised and impressed at how much quicker the dog's body language changes when you take the pressure away rather than increase it.

Unless your dog has only recently developed this problem, and was previously comfortable and actively enjoyed contact with strangers, be careful about the stranger using treats to get the dog to come closer. The chance of a bite is greatly increased. If he stays away, he definitely cannot bite. If you are the owner of a shouting/ swearing dog, avoid scenarios where he can practise this behaviour. Do not put him in situations where he feels he needs to react.

You need to be your dog's bodyguard. Protect him from situations he cannot cope with at the moment. Be super casual in your body language when doing so – everything about how you move has to be saying to him: "I didn't even notice that stranger was scary" – while, at the same time you are creating as much space as he needs to feel OK. It is only by addressing what the dog perceives that we can change his emotional perception and build his confidence.

SUMMING UP

How strangers and visitors are viewed can be very different to how your dog regards his family. By observing his body language during such encounters you will have a good idea of how he feels.

Dogs can find the human race unpredictable and frightening; some certainly think we are quick to show aggression and use threatening techniques. This may have been totally unintentional as far as the human was concerned, but we have to see things from the dog's perspective.

It is only by addressing what the dog perceives that we can change his emotional perception and build his confidence. If this is too hard, taking too long, or is not practical for you or him, get professional assistance from someone who will work on helping you build his confidence, working on his underlying emotional state and not simply focusing on his symptomatic behaviours.

AN EXTREME EXAMPLE OF A LEARNT NEGATIVE ASSOCIATION WITH TREATS

1. Dog:" Scary stranger! Interesting though."
Stiff movement with head downwards while arcing around the stranger. Hackles evident.

2. Dog: "Let's pretend she's not there."
Sniffing even though he's in his own garden.

3. Dog: "Actually this stranger knows a thing or two!"
He has now moved closer, and seems to appreciate the under chin scratch, though his tail ears and back legs tell us he is still concerned.

4. Dog "Uh Oh! I'd love some but I know you'll do something to me."
He has distanced himself to a potentially safer place – but still looks at the treats.

5. Dog: "Let's get out of here."
A return to the stiff movement with head neck and tail lowered as he exits the situation.

6. Dog "Phew! That was a close one!"
Having got to a perceived safe distance, he lip licks and and urinates at the same time.

CONCLUSION

Increasingly we are seeing science and real-life experience merge, which means that our useful understanding of dog behaviour and communication is growing. This never-ending quest to understand these amazing creatures is not only yours, and mine, but that of the entire worldwide pet dog-owning community.

Our human perspective limits us, but we automatically try to interpret and translate a dog's nature – his dogginess – into something we can understand and relate to. As a human we can never know what it is to be a dog – but this just adds to the excitement and intrigue.

Inevitably, there will continue to be misinformed and misguided advice and information, and it can be hard to know what course of action to take. But you are the one who knows your dog – so there is only one question

that need concern you. Could this stress my dog now or in the long-term? If something doesn't sit comfortably with you – forget it. It isn't right for your dog.

If you are able see the clues he gives, and understand what is likely to be difficult for him – you have your evidence. You are in a position to make judgements, and work out how best to proceed. Inevitably there will be times when you have to compromise – but always remember: you chose your dog, and you are responsible for his quality of life.

Your dog holds so many secrets, he has so much more to say – all we need to do is open our eyes. Then you will discover how to make a difference. Your relationship, as close as it is now, will grow even closer. As good as his life is now, it will get even better.

Just look. You'll see.